THE 18/40 RULE

Escaping Autopilot in the Age of AI

Shane Mahoney
Luxury Lifestyle Specialist

ISBN: 979-8-9924188-7-3

Publisher: **Author Writer's Academy**
AWA Literary Agency, United States
Senior Editor: Marjah Simon
www.AWA4Life.com

Cover Design and Illustrations - Author Writer's Academy

Dedication

To Corsten Quinn Mahoney, my son,

you teach me every day how
and why to be a better person.
Your personality lights up my life
with your generosity and kindness.

and to **Christina Diane Ingrassia**, my wife,

you love, support, and are there for me
and our son every day.
You are the best part of my life.
I'm deeply honored and grateful
to have met such an incredible person,
let alone to have the honor of sharing my life with you.

Acknowledgements

I'd like to acknowledge the following people and organizations that I've been honored to share time, ideas, conversations, and thoughts with over the years.

Firstly, my mother, **Maria Mahoney,** you have been an example in my life in so many ways. Your tireless work to keep the family together, to negotiate peace, and to ensure we share the important values from one generation to the next.

To **my father,** you taught me many things, and I hope I've made you proud through the decisions I've made.

To my brother, **Spencer Mahoney,** you are a great dad. I'm proud to see you take control of your life in helping others.

To **my mother-in-law** and **father-in-law**, you are both pretty amazing people. I'm thankful you share time and wisdom with our son.

To my grandmother, **Nonny,** you have been the glue that held our family together through so many rough and challenging times. On behalf of myself, my cousins, the aunties, and everyone who has met you, thank you for being you. You always make me smile!

To **Marjah Simon,** my publisher, for your incredible work teasing out of my brain the most important nuggets in this book. Your work and methods made this process much easier and less scary than I had imagined.

To **Mike 'Megeve' Baudet,** you truly helped me find my calling at a moment when I had little direction or idea of what to do. You generously gave your time (our most valuable asset) to a stranger and helped me see the art of what's possible.

To members and leadership of **Family Mastermind, Board of Advisors,** and Power Room, I thank you for your efforts to bring entrepreneurs together.

And to my friends, Brent Youngs, L.C. Jones, David Fridovich, Don Westerfeld, Ty Crandall, Brett Lane, Marc Ensign, Cory Bergeron, Joel Moyes, Jeannie Pond, Damieon Hulett, Jeremy Sharack, Darren Tamayo, Farhan Rehmani, Daniel Gorman, Amanda Meadows, Marie Grondin, Matt Hunn, Rey Perez, RJ Garbowicz, and so many more, thank you for your years of friendship. Having you all to bounce my ideas off of, or just have someone to talk to, has been invaluable in my life. I love and appreciate you all.

Contents

Letter From The Author

If you're holding this book in your hands, there's a reason. Maybe you're feeling the quiet weight of time passing. Maybe you've hit a moment in life that made you stop and ask, Is this really it? Or maybe you've just realized that despite all the checkboxes you've ticked, something still feels off.

I've been there. And I wrote this because I don't want you to wait until life forces you to ask the hard questions. I want you to ask them now – while you still can.

We all tell ourselves the lie of "someday." But the longer we wait for "someday" to come around, the more likely it is that the window we're waiting for quietly closes without us ever realizing it.

This isn't just a book. It's a wake-up call. A line in the sand. A reminder that life is shorter, more fragile, and more beautiful than we let ourselves believe. We don't have to wait for "someday," not for the perfect moment, not until everything is figured out … Because the truth is, tomorrow isn't promised – not for me, not for you, not for anyone.

My own story isn't without its wake-up calls. I was diagnosed with Parkinson's, and while that news could have changed everything, it didn't shift my worldview. It sharpened it. You see, I've been living with this urgency for decades, long before the diagnosis ever came.

That just added clarity to a belief I've always held close: our time is not guaranteed.

And yet, I see it every day: people living on autopilot, waiting to "get around" to what they really want. They tell themselves they'll travel someday. They'll slow down someday. They'll finally have that big, life-changing adventure … someday.

But then someday slips away.

I've seen dreams deferred until they're no longer possible. I've seen strong people who planned for later, only to find that "later" never came. And those stories stay with me. They're why I don't wait anymore.

So take this as your invitation to live differently – not louder or faster, but more honestly. More intentionally. With the courage to stop chasing someone else's definition of success and start building a life that's actually yours.

You don't need a diagnosis to start doing that. You don't need a crisis. You just need to decide that today is the day you stop waiting.

So I want to challenge you: If you knew exactly how many summers you had left, what would you change right now?

What would you say no to?

What would you make space for?

What dream would you stop deferring?

Because presence is the only real currency we have. And when you show up for your life, fully and unapologetically, you realize something incredible: you've had the power all along to live a life that's rich, meaningful, and entirely your own.

So what are you waiting for?

Shane Mahoney

Introduction

I have dedicated my life to helping people go on out-of-this-world experiences, not once-in-a-lifetime experiences. Why? Because people wait their whole lives for that once-in-a-lifetime experience without really knowing there's a difference between having an ordinary experience and an extraordinary one – one that goes much deeper than the price point.

We only have *one* life. We want to fill that with as many experiences as possible, and that's why at Lugos Travel, we make sure that you have the opportunity to live life to the fullest – one out-of-this-world experience after the next.

Because our time is not guaranteed; presence is the only real currency.

It's categorically cliché, but we have to live every moment like it matters. Every moment, big or small, is important because in every moment, there is the chance for opportunity, the chance to experience life at its fullest.

There are moments in our lives that are there to test our beliefs, and not in some surface-level way, but deep down, asking, "Do you *really* believe what you say you believe?" It's easy to talk a good game, but moments of real pressure reveal just how sure you are of yourself. They show how deep those convictions actually run.

Lately, and perhaps with good reason since my diagnosis, I've noticed myself becoming more emotional than I've typically been.

For a long time, I felt almost robotic, disconnected from deeper emotions, and it turns out that might actually be tied to lower dopamine levels. I didn't feel much day-to-day emotion, but then I'd get hit hard in these strange, unexpected moments – like during movies. It wasn't even always the obvious ones, either. Sure, something like *Inside Out* would have me just completely losing it, a total blubbering mess. But even movies that weren't traditionally tearjerkers, like the end of *Saving Private Ryan* – that scene where he asks if he's been a good man – would leave me wrecked.

I think it's because I'm so introspective. I think about what I'm leaving behind – not just for humanity in some grand sense, but in a personal way. For my kid. For my wife. For the people closest to me. That's the stuff that gets me.

But when it comes to my diagnosis, and how it has shifted the way I view or live life, the truth is that it really hasn't changed my philosophy much at all. I've been thinking about these ideas for over twenty years, more than a quarter of a century. The diagnosis didn't change my thinking; it just reinforced it, sharpened it, made it all more immediate. I always knew there was a ticking clock somewhere in the background; now, I just have a clearer sense of how much time might actually be on it.

And even then, nothing is guaranteed. A lot could happen between now and whatever finish line is out there. Still, the diagnosis does have a way of making you refocus in a hurry.

For instance, this book feels like it came from somewhere else. I knew I had things I wanted to say, but I didn't really know how to organize them, how to focus them, how to avoid writing something that just started every sentence with "I." Because, let's face it, that would make for a boring book. So I sat in my thoughts for a while, distilling them, trying to put them into an organized shape. I definitely knew the core of what I wanted to say; it took some time to get it all together, but, well, you're holding it in your hand, right? It all came together in the end, no more waiting for the perfect time.

The time we have is finite, so why wait?

Getting my diagnosis really drove that point home in a way nothing else could. It was like a switch flipped. I'd love to say I'm going to keep my wits about me for a long time, but the reality is, with Parkinson's, things can change quickly. Some people maintain their faculties for years; others experience a steep decline within two, three, four, or five years. And Parkinson's isn't even the same disease for everybody: for some, it's mostly motor function; for others, it's cognitive; then others experience both. Right now, I don't know exactly what I'm facing. I'm supposed to get a genetic test soon, and I'm about six months out from getting a full referral diagnosis where they can really dig into the details.

At the end of the day, though, my philosophy hasn't wavered. If anything, it feels like everything I believe can be summed up by a line from *The Shawshank Redemption*: **"Get busy living, or get busy dying."** It's so brutally honest. We can't guarantee what happens next. None of us can. But we have *now*. And right now, we can live. Dying is inevitable. The real question is: will the *living* happen?

A World of Questions

When we are young, we are prone to asking hundreds of thousands of questions about everything and anything. We want to know how and why and what and when and where … But at some point, we stop asking so many questions, and when we do, they're not the same kind of questions. Rarely do we go as deep, believing surface-level questions and surface-level answers are sufficient.

However, as you read this book, I want you to start asking deep questions again; I want you to get curious about what I'm saying and about your life. And I want you to think about which questions are most important to you.

For me, the most important question is always Why? Why this, why that – just Why? It's the question I ask about everything, from my actions to my thoughts, to the things that shape my life.

Let me give you an example.

Some people get tattoos because they're free on Friday the 13th. Why? Well, it's another opportunity to add to their ink collection and it's free. But when the "why" is reduced to something so surface-level, it loses its significance. On the other hand, some people get tattoos that have deep personal meaning. These tattoos aren't impulsive; they've been thought through carefully.

They serve as visual reminders of who they are, what they want to be, or moments that shaped their life. The why behind these tattoos is powerful.

The importance of the why changes everything.

For me, the Why is the most important question in everything I do. If I'm going to commit to something, I need to understand why it matters to me. It may not always result in a perfect answer, and the outcome might not always align with my expectations – but that's not the point. What matters is that whatever I do, I want it to be thought out, purposeful. I need to weigh how I really feel about it. Is the juice worth the squeeze?

You'll never really know if all you have are surface-level conversations. It requires a deeper level of connection, a real conversation about what these experiences mean.
There are challenges, of course. If you're someone motivated purely by money, for example, it might be harder to see past that. But that's okay. Not everyone will resonate with the deeper "why." If that's not for you, then find your own reason and pursue that path.

There's no one-size-fits-all approach to living a great life. It's not about traveling or doing something "cool" to prove a point to others. It's about choosing a path that aligns with the questions you find most important, because that's the journey that will mean the most to you.

PART I
The 18/40 Rule
The Wake Up Call

Here's the thing about time: We all pretend we have more of it than we do.

I spent the first 35 years of my life running on autopilot, chasing the next thing, assuming tomorrow was guaranteed. Then someone made me think about how many summers I have left, and it hit me like a freight train. Not because the math was complicated – it wasn't. But because suddenly, time had a number attached to it. A finite, countable number.

That's when everything changed.

Too many of us are operating on the notion that we'll get around to living "someday," but you're about to discover why your time is more precious – and more limited – than you've let yourself believe.

Fair warning: This might feel uncomfortable. It might make you question how you've been spending your days. Good. That's the point. Because once you see time for what it really is – once you understand what the 18/40 Rule means for your life – you can't unsee it.

And that's exactly when you start living differently.

Let's begin with a simple question: *If you knew exactly how many summers you had left, what would you change today?*

Chapter One
Eight Summers Left

"Don't count the days,

make the days count."

– Muhammad Ali

How many times have you had an "a-ha" moment? When suddenly something clicks, the curtain is pulled back, and everything just makes sense? Some things in life just kind of hit you in the gut, while others take their time to be realized. But whether fast or slow, they always result in that switch being flicked – that "a-ha" moment.

For me, there was something that had been on my mind for a while, something I was thinking about constantly but couldn't quite place until it hit me. My "a-ha" moment. Quick and fast. And from that moment came something I call my 18/40 Rule.

It all began when I was 35, early on in my career, and someone asked me how old I was, and when I replied, "35," they casually said, "Oh, so you have 40 summers left." Just hearing that felt like a punch in the gut. Forty summers. It was such a simple statement, yet it felt like the weight of the world was suddenly on my shoulders. At that moment,

I realized that life, in a very real way, was finite.

So, in the 18/40 Rule, the number 40 represents the summers you have left. Once you subtract your childhood – those first 20 or so years of school and growing up under your parents' rules – you're left with about 40 years. And during those 40 years, especially in your 20s and early 30s, you're caught in a cycle. You're working toward retirement, buying a house, paying for a car, having a family, and doing what society expects of you. You get on this hamster wheel without questioning why. Everyone around you is doing the same thing, so it must be the right thing, right?

But that hamster wheel – that inertia – is a dangerous thing. It keeps you moving forward, even when you're not sure of the direction. To some people, this might sound idyllic, but in reality, you're just blindly walking through life, letting things happen *to* you rather than *for* you. And this is the part that starts to resonate when people talk about going through a "midlife crisis." There was a stage in my life when I began to wonder, "Am I going to go through that too?" However, what I realized was that a midlife crisis wasn't just some arbitrary phase. It's the moment when you recognize that the life you've been living hasn't truly been yours. You've followed a path that others laid out for you, and it's led to a place where you wonder: "Is this it?"

In that moment, you face a tough decision: do you continue on the path that feels comfortable but unfulfilling, or do you take a leap into something that challenges you, pushes you out of your comfort zone, and could risk everything you've built?

It might seem a little morbid, but the reality is you have 40 summers to make that decision. 40 summers to build the life you truly want, to make a difference, and to enjoy what life has to offer.

Suddenly, when you think about it this way, it's much harder to choose the path of least resistance. It's much harder to settle for the same old vacation or the same old routine. You begin to see life with a new perspective, realizing that you have very limited time to really experience it fully.

And then comes the other number of the 18/40 Rule: the number 18.

When my son was born, I realized, "Oh, sh*t, I have 18 summers to solidify the relationship that I'm going to have with him for the rest of my life." Just 18. You don't realize how fleeting that time is until you have children of your own. The research is staggering, and it was tough to swallow: when your child turns 18, you will have spent more time with them in that one year than in all the years that follow. And when I thought about that, it made every moment with him feel even more precious.

As of writing this book, I have 8 summers left until he turns 18.

And that number feels even smaller when you really let it sink in. You don't get to have your child as a baby forever. By the time they're four or five, they're starting to form their own memories, their own personality. But there are still moments where you can expose them to new experiences, like the trip I took with my son to Italy when he was four. He doesn't remember much of it, but I know that trip had an impact. It was for me as much as it was for him – and I believe those experiences shaped him, even if only in subtle ways.

But even if you don't have children, the 18/40 Rule is about realizing that time is the most finite thing we have.

We are all searching for meaning. We want our lives to count for something, to leave a mark. But let's face it, in the grand scheme of things, the reality is humbling. The universe is billions of years old, and we're just a speck in it. When you think about it, it's easy to feel insignificant. Even if you make an impact, it's a drop in the ocean compared to the vastness of time. And as a species, we're great at finding ways to diminish our own worth, value, and impact. But here's the thing: while we might never influence the entire course of human history, we can shape the lives of those around us.

Some people, like Bill Gates, have used their wealth and influence to start foundations that are changing the world. Whether you love him or hate him, his work is undeniable.

He took a significant fortune and used it to make a lasting difference. However, there are also people making a difference every day in their communities, in ways that don't necessarily get recognized on a grand scale. People are working in soup kitchens, organizing neighborhood gardens, teaching life skills … And that's the beauty of it – these contributions, no matter how small they seem, add up to something meaningful.

So, the question becomes: What do you want your impact to be? How do you want to be remembered?

Most people want to be remembered for doing something that matters. But that doesn't mean you need to build a massive company or start a global movement. It means finding ways to contribute meaningfully to the lives of those around you. Maybe it's your family, maybe it's your community, but at the end of the day, it's the people you touch that make your life meaningful.

We all want to be remembered well, but the question is, what are you willing to sacrifice for that? Are you willing to spend all your time climbing the corporate ladder, only to realize your kids hardly know you? Are you willing to trade time with your family for the promise of success or recognition?

Here, let me put it another way. This is what I want you to do right now. Not tomorrow. Not "when you have time." Right now.

Take out your phone and open the calculator.

First, calculate your own 40. How old are you? Subtract your age from 75 (that's roughly when most of us hit our "no-go" years). That's how many summers you have left in your prime. For me, at 35, it was 40. What's your number?

Now, if you have kids, calculate your 18. How old is your oldest child? Subtract their age from 18. That's how many summers you have left before they're grown, before your daily influence in their life dramatically decreases.

Write these numbers down. Put them somewhere you'll see them every day. Make them your phone wallpaper. Stick them on your bathroom mirror. Whatever it takes, because once you see these numbers, you shouldn't unsee them.

Look, I'm not trying to scare you. I'm trying to wake you up. The same way someone woke me up when they said, "Oh, so you have 40 summers left." Because after that conversation, I changed everything. Not all at once – I'm not naive. But I started making decisions differently. Instead of asking "Can I afford this?" I started asking "Can I afford NOT to do this?" Instead of saying "Maybe next year," I started saying "Why not now?"

We don't want to get to the end of those 40 summers and when asked, "Was it worth it?", we answer, "Yes, but ... " So stop waiting, and start doing.

Living Out Your Story

My grandmother, my mom's mom, is fascinating, truly one of a kind. They had a good life back in France. My mom was the oldest of four daughters. Their family owned four successful shoe stores in Paris, had an apartment downtown, and a summer house out in the countryside. They were well-off and pretty comfortable, and around the time my mom was eighteen, they started making plans to visit the United States – Boston specifically, where my grandmother's sister and her husband lived. It was meant to be a month-long trip, a way to explore whether they might want to start a new life across the ocean. They were even considering selling the businesses to make the move permanent there and then.

So the whole family – my mom, my aunts, my grandparents – made it to the airport, bags packed, excitement high. But just before they were about to board, my grandfather remembered he was supposed to meet a potential buyer for the stores. In a rush, he convinced my grandmother to sign a blank sheet of paper, saying it would be needed if the deal went through. He promised he'd follow them to Boston in a day or two.

Weeks passed. No word. Nothing.

Worried, my grandmother flew back to France to find out what was going on. When she walked into her apartment, another woman was there – wearing her clothes, living in her house, surrounded by all her things. That woman had legal documents to prove she now owned *everything*. My grandfather had sold it all: the stores, the apartment, the summer house. *Everything*.

My grandmother was left with only a few hundred bucks to her name. No support system. Most of their friends refused to believe her. The family's entire life had evaporated overnight. My mom and her sisters, once private school kids, were now scraping by.

It took two or three years before anyone found my grandfather again. Interpol tracked him down in Miami, blowing through the money with his mistress. But by that point, the damage was done.

My grandmother had it rough, but being the amazing badass woman she was, she stayed vibrant throughout it all. She remarried – twice, actually, to the same man. She made the most of it. She traveled the world, flew on the Concorde, lived in more places than you can count, and in her later years, she became a seamstress for luxury brands like Chanel, doing expert alterations for the wealthy. She found a way to carve out her own independence, even after having everything stolen from her.

She's always been someone who loves life: champagne, caviar, dancing … Every Christmas Eve, my mom throws a big party, full of food, laughter, and vodka, and my grandmother loves it.

But a couple of years ago, when she was around ninety-three, she ended up in the hospital. She was feeling sorry for herself, and honestly, it was hard to watch. She couldn't dance anymore, couldn't drink or eat much of what she loved when she partied because her blood pressure would spike too fast. It felt like all the pleasures she'd cherished were being taken away.

I sat with her one day and said, "Nonny, when you get out of here, let's throw a party. We'll invite everyone: your kids, grandkids, cousins. We'll have champagne, caviar, music. You'll drink as much as you want, eat whatever you want, and we'll celebrate life, however long we have left." The idea would be to go out with a bang, to finish intentionally, to celebrate, not mourn. That's how I'd want to do it, too – live fully, not fearfully. But she doesn't want to do anything like that, and that's her choice. She has certainly lived a full life, in my opinion, and to be honest, she's stubborn and tough; she'll probably outlive us all. She is 95 and still going!

But that conversation with Nonny really got me thinking about how I want to live out my own story. Why does that approach to celebrate until the end resonate so much for me?

Because it's about control. It's about directing my life rather than clinging to the hope that it might stretch endlessly. I have a very keen sense of the finality of it all, especially nowadays, and I'm not afraid of it. I don't believe in Heaven, or anything religious like that. But I believe in energy: It's neither created nor destroyed.

On the simplest, most cellular level, we're carbon. When we die, our matter feeds the earth, the trees, the cycle of life. Maybe that's not reincarnation in the traditional sense, but it's a kind of continuation, and I find comfort in that. I don't need a specific outcome. I don't need promises. I'm okay with becoming part of something else.

I want to influence what I can, while I'm here, but without clinging to what happens after.

So what's the difference between that philosophy and just living like a reckless rock star: partying, drinking, sex, drugs, nihilism? I've known people like that. Honestly, at points in my life, I've had shades of it myself. It's like, what's the point? If we want to live to our fullest, then why the hell not? Who cares what anyone thinks, right?

But for me, there is a point.

It's about the ripples.

By living truly full lives, can we create ripples that make someone else's life better? And it doesn't have to be something grand; we can't change the whole world, but through our actions, we can create small changes that sometimes have the biggest impact. Telling a stranger that their outfit is incredible. Giving someone a smile. Saying hello to a passerby. You don't know when one small moment could be the catalyst that changes someone's whole trajectory.

We can't control everything, but we can control what kind of energy we put out into the world. And to me, that's enough.

So ask yourself, what kind of energy do you want to put out into the world? And once you have an answer, pick one thing – just one – that you've been putting off that can help you to release that energy out into the world. Maybe it's starting that business, taking that sabbatical, or just taking your kid on that camping trip you keep promising … Whatever it is, I want you to take one concrete step toward it TODAY – not tomorrow.

Because the 18/40 Rule only works if you do something with it.

Your numbers are ticking down whether you act or not. The only question is: What are you going to do about it?

The Art of Asking Questions

I know this chapter might have stirred up some uncomfortable feelings. Good. Sit with them for a minute.

Ask yourself the following reflection questions:

1. **What does the "18/40 Rule" awaken in you?**
   Does it inspire urgency, or does it trigger fear, motivation, or something else? Why?

2. **What does a "full life" even mean to you?**
   Be honest, does your current lifestyle align with that definition?

3. **Think about your last real "a-ha" moment.**
   What did it reveal about your life? More importantly, what did it actually change because of it?

4. **Are you living your life on autopilot right now? *Really think about it.***
   Are you consciously choosing your path, or are you just following the one that was laid out for you?

5. **What have you already sacrificed in the pursuit of success or security? Your time with family? Your health? Your dreams?**
   ... And here's the hardest question: Was it worth it?

These aren't rhetorical questions. These are the questions that, if you answer them honestly, will change how you live the rest of your summers.

Remember: Everyone dies, but not everyone truly lives.

The choice is yours.

Chapter Two
A Good Life, But Not a Full One

"Most men lead lives

of quiet desperation

and go to the grave with

the song still in them."

– Henry David Thoreau

Aside from the obvious, what I've felt more sharply recently is just how little time there really is to f*ck around. This is something I've always known, but maybe due to my current situation, I've become so much more aware of how many people live their lives like tomorrow is guaranteed. They go to bed every night assuming they'll wake up with the same energy, the same family, the same job, the same circumstances. As if everything about their life is a given. But no matter how much we want or believe this to be the case, the reality is that everything can change, and much faster than we think.

Do you remember those numbers you calculated in the last chapter? Your 40 summers, your 18 with your kids? Most people don't know those numbers, or they ignore them completely. They either live in a sort of ignorant bliss or have a momentary pang or urgency and then go right back to living the same comfortable life they've always lived.

And look, I get it. Comfortable isn't bad. Comfortable is … comfortable. But comfortable isn't *full*. And that's the problem.

For years now, I've watched people who have the means, the mode, the ability, and even the will to go do something, to go see the world, stay where they are. They live their lives comfortably, some even living really good lives. But good doesn't always equate to full. Living a full life means living a life where you are ready, willing, and excited to take hold of the opportunities that come your way – you're willing to be uncomfortable. Too many people, for one reason or another, are not, and they let themselves be held back by the smallest things. It's not the big obstacles that stop them; it really is the tiny stuff.

I had a client who came to me to book a vacation around the time he was about to turn eighty. He was a retired attorney, and he had always wanted to go to London, specifically to visit the Royal Courts of Justice. He had made plans to go around 2001, but after 9/11 happened, he deferred his dream – and kept deferring it for nearly a quarter of a century. By the time he finally decided to go, there were accommodations we had to make. He was still mobile, but not as he would have been twenty-five years earlier. However, we were able to put everything in place for him to go and have an out-of-this-world experience, and he did.

He got to have the experience he had dreamed of for so long, and I was so honored to be able to make that happen for him. Yet, what stayed with me more than his praise and feedback from the trip was the thought of how much more he had let pass him by. He had the income. He had the desire. He could have gone on this trip at any time. So why didn't he?

It makes me wonder about what else he might have put off in his life. How many other places did he want to visit that he just never made it to – and maybe never will – because of "some reason"? And how many more are there out there just like him?

Another client comes to mind, one whose story hit differently. They have a grandchild they adore and take care of a couple of days a week, but one of their bucket-list dreams was to take the trans-Canadian railway trip, staying at the iconic Fairmont Banff Springs Hotel, the beautiful "Castle in the Rockies."

Timing the trip was tricky. Their daughter had a very specific window for vacation, and lining it up with theirs was almost a miracle. When they finally came to me, we managed to nail the dates, even with limited availability. We booked them a completely custom, private trans-Canadian experience; however, the one thing we couldn't get? A room at the Fairmont Banff Springs. It was fully booked. Instead, we arranged for them to stay at another

Fairmont property – literally just across the mountain, same distance from town, same views, same management company, same everything except the architecture and the name.

And they said no to the trip. They said, "We'll just do it next year."

I didn't say it out loud, but in my head, all I could think was, *Will you, though?*

It wasn't even that they had stayed at the Banff Springs before and were sentimental about it. They hadn't. They just knew the name and thought that's where they *should* go. And sure, I get that a hotel can be part of the experience. But it's not *the* experience.

It's almost like a trap – one that too many people fall into – thinking that travel, or anything for that matter, is a once-in-a-lifetime opportunity. That if every single detail isn't perfect, it's not worth doing at all. And because of that, they miss out on what life is really offering them. Never sacrifice the good on the altar of the perfect.

Here's an exercise I want you to try. Think about something you've been putting off – not for 25 years maybe, but for longer than you should have. Got it? Good.
Now ask yourself: What's the real reason you haven't done it?

If you're like most people, you'll start with the surface excuses: money, time, work commitments. But dig deeper. What are you really afraid of? Losing control? Looking foolish? Discovering you can't handle it?

Write down your real reason. Not the excuse you tell others, but the fear you whisper to yourself at 3 AM.

After years of watching people defer their dreams, I've learned that it's never about the Fairmont Banff Springs Hotel. It's never about the perfect conditions. It's about the story we tell ourselves about what we deserve, what we're capable of, what's "reasonable" for someone like us.

One of my aims in writing this book was to try to help more people understand that. I want as many people as possible to *experience* life. I want them to invest in themselves, in their experiences, in their opportunities ... Because when they do that, they live life to the fullest. They create space for themselves, for their partners, for their families, in ways they never had before.

But to do that, you need to lean into the moment. When life nudges you – when it tells you to chill, to breathe, to experience something – listen.

Some of my favorite memories from travel have nothing to do with checking big boxes off a list.

In Milan, in front of the Duomo, there's a massive, paved square with all the tourists buzzing around with their selfie sticks, trying to capture the perfect moment. Right next to the square is a little museum café on the second floor, looking down over everything. I get a coffee every time I go there and I just … *watch*. No rushing. No agenda. Just a coffee, a seat, a view, and the feeling of being alive in a beautiful moment. And it didn't come from rushing around to "see the sights" or obsessing over whether every little thing was perfect. It came from just being *present*.

What Are You Doing with Your Time?

Many of us don't make time for life, not really. We treat time like it's an enemy to be conquered, something to outwork and outrun. Every major invention over the last hundred years – vacuum cleaners, cars and planes, hot water heaters, phones, artificial intelligence – has been about saving time. Yet somehow, we're still more "time-starved" than ever. We save time constantly … But what are we doing with it?

We have the same number of hours as everyone else in the world. The real difference is how we use them. And honestly, we're not using them well.

Let's do some brutal math that'll probably piss you off.

You work 8 hours a day, minimum. Add an hour commute each way. That's 10 hours. Sleep for 7 hours. That's 17. You've got 7 hours left for everything else: breakfast, dinner, shower, helping kids with homework, walking the dog, laundry, and maybe – maybe – 30 minutes to actually live.

Now multiply that by 5 days a week, 50 weeks a year, for 40 years.

Congratulations!

You've just calculated how much of your life you're trading for a paycheck.

Still think you've got plenty of time?

It's crazy to think about, but in medieval times, peasants and serfs – people we assume worked themselves to death – only labored an average of 150 days a year. There were natural seasons when you couldn't plow fields or harvest crops, and so you did other things. You lived. You built relationships. You engaged in community life.

Today, we brag about working 80-hour weeks like it's a badge of honor. But that's not what life is supposed to be about. That's not living. That's competing in a game where the prize is burnout. Think about it, by the time you get home from work, how much time do you *really* have?

You still have to make dinner, maybe shower, maybe get changed, throw on a load of laundry, take the dog for a walk, feed the cat, unwind, relax, and then still be in bed at a good time to start the cycle all over again the next day. And if you have kids, then you lose even more time getting through their nighttime routine as well as your own.

You come home from work fried, only to then fry yourself some more. Honestly, I can't blame anyone who just wants to "veg out" and crash in the evenings.

We have an awful relationship with time, especially in the States, and it's because of that poor relationship that we fall into bad habits and comfort.

For example, when it comes to planning a vacation, it's like a cloud builds over you. You *know* you should spend time together, you *know* you don't get much time with your kids, you know it's important, you *know* a vacation is sorely needed … But at 9:00 PM after a long day? You're *spent*. You don't want to make more decisions.

Where are we gonna go? What are we gonna do? How will it work? How much will it cost?

It's pure decision paralysis. The more you have to think about, the easier it is to just say, "Screw it," and crawl into bed.

So what I've seen is that people end up going on vacations where they've already been. Because it's easy. They know what to expect. They know it won't be bad – maybe not amazing, but certainly not bad. Or they book cruises because it's one decision, done. One-and-done planning. Or they go to an all-inclusive resort: show up, dip your feet in the pool, eat at the buffet, brain off.

It's an escape. And there's nothing wrong with wanting a break.

But what I find upsetting is that there's no *enrichment*. No *discovery*. No *challenge* to your beliefs or your systems.

There's no expansion. It's an empty experience. You just get spoon-fed at the trough, whether it's at the all-inclusive or on the cruise. And you might be saying, "Well, Shane, isn't that what vacation is for? Just vegging out and recharging so you can get back to work?"

Sure. For a lot of people, it is. But think about it, and I mean *really* think about it. How many people actually allow themselves time to recharge, even on vacation? How many of you reading this book can say with 100% confidence that when you go away, you unplug and immerse yourself in the experience for 24 hours every day you're away?

Most people are still tied to the life they're trying to escape from. So it becomes an opportunity cost.

Every vacation you repeat, every experience you don't stretch into something new, you're using up these finite, precious moments in your life. And five, ten years later, will you even be able to tell which trip was which? Or will it all blur together?

It's like living in the movie Groundhog Day. If all you ever do is go to the same resort, with the same people, for the same experience, year after year – that's a huge, missed opportunity. Now, you can still love a place. You could even go back every five years, right? But it's a big world. There's so much cool stuff to see and do. And honestly, I don't even think it's just about seeing and doing things.

What I find so interesting about travel is seeing how other people solve those same common problems. What do they do differently?

You notice all these tiny things – how other cultures tackle the same everyday issues – and it adds so much perspective to your own life. You don't have to have everything figured out, but you pick up little tips and tricks. It's the same with business masterminds, right? It's not like one person is going to revolutionize your business overnight, but you'll hear one little idea over here, a small shift over there, and suddenly, you're thinking about your own life or work in a completely different way.

When people ask me what I've gained the most from traveling, it's hard to point to just one thing. It's not one moment, or one place, or one idea. It's everything. Travel has colored how I see the world, how I treat people, and even how I run my business. It's reshaped my thinking in ways that I don't even fully realize until I'm confronted with them in daily life.

My wife, Christina, would be the first to tell you: I just think differently. We've been together eleven years, married nearly as long, and she's seen it firsthand. When you spend enough time outside the bubble you grew up in, you start noticing all the unnecessary weight people carry around – the dogma, the assumptions, the rigid beliefs about how life is "supposed" to be and how our time is "supposed" to be spent.

All of these things are metaphysical sacks that we carry with us all the time, and they are *heavy*. But most people carry these sacks without ever questioning if they need to. If they just put them down, even for a minute, they'd realize how much lighter, easier, and freer life could feel.

So, be cool. Don't rush. Spend time, *real* time, doing things you wouldn't normally do. Push yourself. Try things you think you don't like.

It's amazing how often people say they hate something, like wine, for instance, when really, they've just never had good wine. There's a world of difference between the cheap stuff and something crafted with love and pride. The same goes for beer. I was talking with a guy at the gym recently, and he asked if I drink beer. I told him, "Yeah, but probably not in the way you're thinking." Because once you've been to Belgium and tasted real beer, it's hard to come back to mass-produced American lagers. It's the difference between wanting to just get drunk and wanting to truly experience something.

This sense of pride and craftsmanship shows up everywhere once you start noticing it. Even in something as small as breakfast. In the United States, you go to a continental breakfast at almost any hotel, and it's a sad little buffet of stale pastries, over-ripe fruit, bagels, and cheap cereal. Hamster food would be a better alternative sometimes.

But walk into any hotel in Europe and you'll find fresh cheeses, cured meats, honeycomb, pastries, and chocolate-covered orange peel – *every day.* There's pride in the everyday, in the little details, and it completely shifts how you think about quality, about care, about what matters.

What Will You See
When You Look Back?

"In the end, we only regret
the chances we didn't take,
the relationships we were afraid to have,
and the decisions we waited too
long to make."

– Lewis Carroll.

Eventually, everybody's going to look back, and when they do – because they will - they're going to feel either pride or regret. There's no escaping it. We're going to have a feeling one way or another, and the finality of the moment will hit us like a ton of bricks because suddenly, we realize we've either used our time wisely … or we didn't.

I think the biggest thing I can say to you is this: You can't escape yourself. So many of us try. It's why we work all the time, why we distract ourselves with Instagram, TikTok, whatever – we're trying to escape our own thoughts. Trying to avoid thinking about the bad sh*t that's gone wrong, the things we could be doing better, the stuff we're afraid of. But we can only run away for so long. At some point, there's no escape. You have to face yourself.

And that's when you have to stand up and face it. And usually, the stuff that scares you the most is exactly the stuff you should lean *into*. As soon as you realize, "I'm scared," you should be asking: "What am I scared of? And how can I go right at it?"

Close your eyes for a second. Picture yourself at 80, sitting in a rocking chair, looking back at your life. What do you see?

The promotions you got? The emails you answered at 11 PM? The vacations you didn't take because work was "too busy"? OR do you see the time you said "f*ck it" and took your kid out of school for a random adventure? The anniversary trip where you splurged on the suite with the view? The job you quit to start that business everyone said was crazy?

Nobody gets to their deathbed and wishes they'd been more careful. Nobody regrets the chances they took. They regret the ones they *didn't*.

In my life, I was scared of going rollerblading 50 miles an hour down a mountain, weaving between traffic. On one side: a 200-foot cliff. On the other: a rock wall. Plus, every hundred yards, a huge drainage grate that I had to jump over on rollerblades at top speed. Every time I landed, my skates would get a little squirrely. It was nuts. It was the only way to get down the mountain fast enough to play basketball with all my friends. But I loved it.

I wasn't scared of the outcome – I was just *in it*. And that made the possibly poor judgment worth it.

And that's kind of how I've lived my life since. I don't have an attachment to what happens after the moment. I just want to be true to who I want to be right now. If you're sure of yourself – if you trust your instincts – most of the time, you'll be okay. (Disclaimer: *You might get hit by a car ... or you might have the ride of your life.*)

I was never prone to making good judgments, but I was prone to taking chances. In college, I'd even grab onto the backs of cars, Marty McFly-style, to catch rides around campus. I actually got ticketed for it once. The cops were hilarious, standing there flipping through their book of violations, totally unsure what to charge me with. Eventually, they settled on giving me a "student non-academic citation," and I knew immediately: *I'm getting out of this.*

When I appealed, I just stood up and said, "Look, under no circumstances am I defending this as smart. It's stupid, it's dangerous, but it's not illegal. There's no rule against it." And of course, they dropped the charges.

I see so many people living with fear. I really think fear drives most people – I *know* it does at least on some level. People are scared of what might happen, scared of what others might think, scared of change, scared of the unknown.

And to me, the crazy part is the world just isn't that scary. It's not as terrifying as everyone builds it up to be in their heads.

I've had genuinely scary experiences. I was carjacked at knifepoint once. That was real fear, no doubt about it, and in the moment, it was terrifying. But when I look at the way most people operate day-to-day, carrying around guns or constantly preparing for disaster, it just doesn't match the reality of how often those moments actually happen. People justify it by thinking, *Well, something might happen,* and they want to be ready for it. But I categorically reject that mindset.

For one thing, I'm a damn good marksman. At ranges, I've outshot people who were supposed to be way better than me – trained police officers, military instructors, even experts. I don't even own a gun, and yet every time I've been taken to a range by those professionals, I've handled their own weapons better than they did. I know exactly what it feels like to shoot a gun, and I also know exactly what it feels like to be in a real high-stress, life-threatening situation.

The idea that you're going to have any meaningful control in those moments – that you're going to calmly pull out a weapon, accurately aim it, make a perfect decision under pressure without hitting anyone innocent – is just a fantasy. It's a complete falsehood. In crowded areas, under extreme stress, it's incredibly unlikely you'll be able to perform the way you imagine.

Even the people who are trained, people who are *supposed* to be ready, often panic when things get real. You only have to look at places like Uvalde to understand that. When fear takes over, all the preparation and bravado in the world doesn't necessarily matter. It's just scary as hell.

Facing your own mortality, truly facing it, is one of the scariest things a person can go through. And if you're not prepared for that moment, it's even worse. But here's the catch: If you spend your whole life constantly bracing for the worst, constantly preparing for fear, all you're really doing is conditioning yourself to live in fear. You're priming yourself to see danger around every corner, and it starts to bleed into every part of your life.

You stop taking chances. You don't try anything new. You don't go after the opportunities you want. You don't even try to get a dinner reservation at the restaurant you love because fear, in a hundred little ways, keeps holding you back. It becomes a loop – fear, fear, fear, fear, fear – and it shapes every decision you make until you're not even living anymore. You're just surviving, trapped forever in the outcome of "What if ... "

But then people ask, "If I'm not focused on the outcome, then what am I focused on? If I detach from the results, won't I just drift?" They get stuck themselves in another form of fear and don't realize that that's not what detachment means.

Detachment doesn't mean you stop caring. It doesn't mean you stop doing your best. It just means you don't tie your worth to whether or not it works out. You're still showing up. Still pushing. Still swinging for the fences. You just stop believing that *the result* is the proof of your value. Because you know it's not.

You may do everything right, and it still might not work out. That's okay. That's life. You're not saying, "I have no goals." You're saying, "I'll do what's in my control, I'll take this chance, and let go of the rest."

Failure only exists the moment you stop trying.

Ask Dwayne Johnson. He had seven bucks left when he started his career. Or John Boyega. $43 in his bank account when J.J. Abrams told him he got Star Wars. He spent $35 just to get to that meeting.

That's what focus looks like. That's what belief looks like. That's what it looks like when you detach yourself from the outcome, from fear, and start living your life fully.

The Art of Asking Questions

You might be feeling overwhelmed right now. Like I just dumped a lot on you. If so, that means you're actually thinking about this stuff instead of just reading it.

So, while I have your attention, let me ask you:

1. **How many beliefs about how life "should" look are actually yours, and how many did you inherit from your parents, your culture, that guidance counselor who said you'd never amount to anything?**
   Are any of them quietly limiting your freedom, joy, or willingness to try new things?

2. **When was the last time you leaned into something that scared you? What did you learn about yourself from it?**
   Can you even remember?

3. **Think about all the time-saving devices in your life. Your dishwasher, your smartphone, your Roomba. Where did all that saved time go?**
   I'm betting it didn't go toward living fuller.

4. **When was the last time you leaned into something that scared you – and what did you learn about yourself from it?**
    How did that experience shape your growth or perspective?

5. **This is the one that will really get you: If you knew you had five years left to live, what would you stop postponing immediately?**
    Got your answer? Good. Now tell me: Why the hell haven't you already done it?

These questions aren't comfortable. They're not supposed to be. Comfortable is what got you here – living a good life, but not a full one.

Chapter Three
Redefining Rich

"Being rich is having money;

being wealthy is having time."

– Margaret Bonnano

A lot of people have a really hard time treating themselves. Even when it's something simple. Even when they can absolutely afford it.

Whenever I arrange a vacation, for example, I like to include a private car to pick them up at their house and take them to the airport because I genuinely believe the vacation should start the minute you leave your front door, not when you finally get to your destination. But, as you can probably imagine, a lot of people push back. They say, "Oh, that's not necessary. We'll just drive ourselves." And I'm thinking, *Of course it's not necessary.* I know they know how to drive. That's not what it's about.

By doing those things, I'm trying to help you see and feel that you deserve this. It's about realizing you've worked your f*cking a** off, that you've put the time, the energy, the blood, the sweat, the tears … You've earned this moment where you can just let go and be taken care of.

And let's be honest, there's no U-Haul pulling up behind the hearse. So if you're not going to enjoy some of it while you're here, *what the f*ck are you even doing it for?*

In the last two chapters, we talked about how limited our time really is. The 18/40 Rule. The difference between a good life and a full one. Now let's talk about what most people think they need before they can start living that full life: money.

Now, I'm not going to tell you money doesn't matter. That's bullshit. Money matters. But not in the way you think it does.

One of my friends from college used to say something that's always stuck with me. We were broke back then – scraping every penny together to take a trip – and she would say, "We're independently wealthy, and we do this all the time." It was our mantra; we redefined what it meant to be rich. Because life is about giving yourself permission to enjoy the moment, to trust that it's okay, that you're allowed – that's what helps you seize opportunity and makes your life rich.

Right now, I'm deeply committed to figuring out who I am and how I can best serve my family. How can I find those little moments to really show up for them? How can I learn? How can I actually learn the art of *not working*, so I can help others find that too?

This has been on my mind for a long time. My mom is still working, a complete workaholic, and my dad was the same; he was a truck driver for many years, and even though he's retired now, that workaholic mentality never really left him. It wasn't long after I got out of college and landed my first couple of jobs that I realized: *Oh my God, I'm a workaholic too!*

I was clocking 80-plus hour weeks. Although honestly, it wasn't real work all the way through. It was being *at* work. It was hanging around the water cooler, long lunch breaks, cornhole games at the office – all these little distractions that break up the day. But there was still this underlying expectation to be there, to show up, to grind. I realized pretty quickly that I was predisposed to locking myself in an office and staying there all day without a second thought. There's always something more to do, some new thing to chase, some reason to keep the machine moving.

But when my son Corsten was born, everything changed. His grandparents could only watch him three days a week, so that left two days where it was just me and him. I became Dad-Daycare.

In my head, I had it all figured out: He's under two, I'll feed him, check on him, and get back to work. I can already hear you laughing at me, because you know that that's not how it works. And if you have kids of your own, you know it's not even close. So you'll be unsurprised to hear that reality hit hard day one.

So what my life became was this grind where on Mondays, Wednesdays, and Fridays, I'd work like a maniac. I'd go to bed at midnight or one in the morning. Then, when Corsten woke up at 6:00 AM, I'd be up with him, taking care of him all day. After dinner and bath time, when he was finally down around 7:30 PM, I'd go back to work until 1:00 AM, sleep a few hours, and start again. And I did that for two straight years. Just grinding. Making it all somehow work.

But during that time, I started to see that this massive list of "urgent" work tasks I thought I had to do, most of them didn't really matter. Some days, I'd just say, "You know what? Screw it. I'm not doing that today." And shockingly, nothing bad happened. The business didn't collapse. The world didn't end.

It was a revelation.

Here, take a moment and try this:

- Write down everything you think you "have to" do this week. *Everything.* The report due Friday. The dentist appointment. The client presentation. Your kid's soccer practice. All of it.
- Next to each item, write "Fixed" or "Flexible." Be honest. That report might have a deadline, but could it be pushed a day if your kid was sick? That's flexible. Your kid's birthday? Fixed.

- For every "Flexible" item, ask yourself: "What would actually happen if I didn't do this?" Not what you fear would happen. What would ACTUALLY happen.
- Now, the hardest part … Pick three flexible items and don't do them. Just don't. See what happens.

I guarantee you'll discover that most of what we call "urgent" is just noise. And when you clear out the noise, you make space for what actually matters.

We create so much "urgent" and "important" work for ourselves that, if we were honest, we could just let go. I started focusing only on the core things that actually mattered. I learned to ignore the noise – or, eventually, to hire help for the parts that didn't need my hands directly.

Sure, maybe the business didn't grow as fast as it could have. But what I got in exchange was way more valuable: a real relationship with my son. That's why even now, years later, there's no question who he wants to tuck him in at night.

In contrast, there was this guy I knew who had a young kid of his own. I would watch him interact with his daughter; she would come into his office and he'd immediately shoo her away. "Go out. I got work to do." Always working. Always too *busy.* It's that old "Cats in the Cradle" song playing out in real life: Don't worry, I promise to connect later, once the work is done.

But later isn't promised. And even if it is, the damage is already done by then.

If you think of "providing" only as putting a roof over their heads or food on the table, you're missing the point. That's survival. Provision isn't just the stuff you buy; it's the presence you give. It's the investment into their soul – and your own. It's the difference between an AI-generated trip itinerary and a *real* experience curated by someone who cares. One fills a checklist. The other fills your heart. And when you do the other, that's when you know you're truly rich.

Impossible to "I'm Possible"

When you hear about something that seems impossible, it's easy to think it can't be done. But in my experience, what's impossible is not trying. I'm not going to get everything right, but I always believe there's a way, and I just have to figure out how to make it happen.

For example, I have this client who takes his four sons on a guy's trip every year. I absolutely love working with him. He's super cool, and he and his wife also do trips together. They just went to Paris for New Year's. We were able to arrange a couple of really cool experiences. His wife wanted to get into this restaurant called Gigi, which Jennifer Lopez had recently named as her favorite spot. I told her, "No problem. It's usually booked a year and a half in advance, but I'll get you in." Sure enough, I made it happen.

Now, she didn't book it that far in advance – she had actually tried to book it herself just two weeks prior, but it wasn't going to happen. So, she reached out to me, and I worked some magic to get her in. When she walked into Gigi, she was blown away. She called me up and said, "Shane, I've been on a lot of trips with you, but I had no idea you could do this. That was amazing!" Then, she asked, "Can you get me a reservation at the Louis Vuitton Café?" I said, "Sure, it's booked a year and a half in advance, but I'll take care of it."

And I did. I made the impossible possible.

Most of us have "possibility blindness." We can't see solutions because we've already decided they don't exist. However, most "impossible" things are just puzzles we haven't solved yet. The trick is believing there's a solution before you can see it.

Most people never achieve their goals because they don't create the mental space to consider all the possibilities. People are often resolute, sure that they know the answer, but that's where problems arise. We tend to forget that there are many answers, not just one. Someone once said, "I'm absolutely 100% sure that I'm 50% possibly right." I tend to agree. If I'm sure of something, it's probably because I've already made an assumption that's not entirely accurate. There's rarely just one way to do something.

So, how can you look at your life from a new perspective? How can you open yourself up to "What's next?"

First, you need to take a step back and make a change. The problem doesn't come from knowing what to do; it's about not being specific enough or not having a clear outcome attached to anything. Sometimes it's just about zigging when you've been zagging. It's about doing something different, something unexpected.

Imagine you've been walking one way your whole life – what if you just turned around and walked the other direction? Or better yet, what if you skipped for a change? The other day, I just skipped. It felt good. In elementary school, did you ever climb up on top of your desk just to look at the room from a different angle? Or maybe not in school, but did you ever do the same thing with a tree? How did the world suddenly look when it felt like you were looking at it from hundreds of feet in the air? That simple shift in perspective was powerful, right?

Nowadays, I do this through meditation, stepping back and trying to be a bystander in my own life. It's not easy. It takes focus, training, and time, but it's something you can cultivate. The most important part is truly believing that things are possible.

When I first met my wife Christina, she believed so many things were impossible. For instance, she thought it was impossible to walk into a restaurant with a huge line and get in right away by just palming a couple of bucks. She'd be like, "No way, that can't happen." But I'd say to her, "Just hold the possibility that it *could* happen, and if it doesn't, it's fine." It's all about keeping that open mind. If one way doesn't work, it's not a failure, just a signal that you need to try a different way next time.

It would be great if more people realized that while money is important, it's not everything. At the end of the day, if you've ever read about hospice nurses and what they witness near the end of people's lives, you'll see a common thread. Not once do they hear someone say, "I wish I'd spent more time at the office. Instead, they hear, "I wish I'd spent more time with my family, or I wish I'd done this or that." But never is it about "I'm so glad I had $10,000 more in my savings account instead of $10." At the end of the day, money doesn't matter as much as the relationships and experiences you've built.

If I were going to pass something on to my kid, it wouldn't be just a bank account or a house. Those things are great, don't get me wrong, but I'd much rather pass on the mental game – the mindset that allows him to think flexibly, to adapt, and to go after what he wants in life. An adaptable mind is far more valuable than anything material.

Good, Bad ... No Difference

I lived in Borneo when I was two. Then, a few years later, we moved to Perth, Australia, where I spent three years of my childhood while my dad worked on an exploratory oil ship in the Indian Ocean. He'd be gone two weeks, home two weeks – rinse and repeat. But back then, they didn't have the equipment they do now – no GPS, no fancy modeling – they just picked a point and said, "Let's try over here." No oil? "Okay, try over there."

They never struck oil, and eventually, the company went under. Because of that, we lost our visa to stay in Australia. My parents would have stayed forever, I think. But instead, we had to pack up and return to the States.

For a while, we were in West Palm, and eventually my dad landed a job in Lakeland. I was in fourth grade when we moved, and I was the weirdest kid in the whole damn county. Still with traces of an Australian accent, I'd been around the world four, maybe five times. Most of the other kids had never left their zip code. In every instance, I just thought, *What am I doing here?*

At the time, it all felt like a mess. A failed job. Losing our home. Getting uprooted. But years later, I realized: if they had found oil, none of my life as it is now would've happened. We wouldn't have moved. I wouldn't have met Christina. I wouldn't have had my son.

In our lives, we tend to label everything as either good or bad the moment it happens. But in reality, you can only truly know what something means with the fullness of time. There's an old Chinese proverb that sticks in my mind:

A farmer's horse runs away, and the villagers come over, all sympathetic. "What terrible luck," they say. But the farmer just shrugs and replies, "We'll see." The next day, the horse returns and brings back a whole group of wild horses with it. The villagers, now amazed, come back saying, "What good fortune!" Again, the farmer says, "We'll see." Then his son tries to break one of the wild horses, falls off, and breaks his arm. The villagers return, shaking their heads: "So unlucky." And again, the farmer replies, "We'll see." A few days later, the army comes through town, conscripting every able-bodied young man to go to war, but the farmer's son is spared because of his broken arm … And so it goes on and on.

The moral of the story is non-attachment, about letting go of the immediate impulse to label every event as good or bad. Something that feels like a loss today may set the stage for something much greater tomorrow. However, we also have to be wary of want.

Wanting itself is often the root of suffering. When you get what you want, you immediately begin wanting something else. When you don't get what you want, that's another version of suffering. But that's where the tension lies.

Should we want things at all? Isn't it natural to have goals, whether financial, personal, or relational? I think the answer is yes, but there's a distinction worth making.

For example, I do have financial goals. But more than anything, what I truly want is for my son to be prepared for life. And that's not really about an outcome, it's about equipping him with a mindset.

When I was younger, especially in my early 20s, I was crushing those material goals. I could've provided a house, college tuition, clothes, food – all the basics a parent is supposed to provide. But when I had my son at 37, I realized I had something more valuable to give than just stability. For the first time in my life, I had a worldview I wanted to pass on. A way of thinking. A way of being.

That's what I call "the mental game."

For anyone wondering what I mean by "mental game," it starts with simple awareness. My son is still innocent. He believes everyone could be a friend. He sees an animal and wants to help. That kind of empathy is beautiful, and I want to nurture it – but I also want him to understand that not everyone is who they seem. Not everyone who is kind is a friend, and not everyone who is firm or critical is an enemy. These are mental distinctions that help him navigate life more effectively.

I want him to grasp that *what happens* matters far less than *how you think about* what happens. The circumstance is often beyond your control, but your mindset – that's yours to own. It's in the minor shifts, the little changes in perspective, that the greatest power lies. So, whether good or bad, have the ability to pause and say, "We'll see."

I know what you're thinking: *Great philosophy, Shane, but I'm dealing with real problems right now. My business is struggling. My relationship is falling apart. My health is shot. How does "we'll see" help me?*

Fair question. Shift your mindset. Ask a different question.

Right now, you're in the middle of your story. You don't know if this chapter is the one where everything falls apart or the one where the hero discovers their strength. You literally cannot know. And that's the point. We cannot control everything in our lives, and we're not meant to. But what we can control is how we respond to this moment.

So if your business is failing, instead of panicking about what you're losing or what you might lose, ask yourself: "What is this situation making possible that wasn't possible before?" If you're struggling to keep a relationship afloat, ask: "What is this telling me about what I want in a relationship?" If your health is suffering, ask, "What is this telling me about how I've been living, and what changes am I now being invited to make?"

Suddenly, you start to shift, you give yourself time, and you find the motivation to try something completely different. A "disaster" can lead to something you never expected, and it's rarely another disaster.

So whatever you're going through right now, try asking: "What is this making possible?" "What is this helping me realize?" "What is this telling me I need to change?" Because I guarantee there's something. You just can't see it yet.

R.O.I.

The world is obsessed with metrics; we are all looking for a return on investment. But what we should be looking for is a return on intimacy, a return on connection, a return on relationships, and a return on life.

I've had clients do amazing things for their families, one that comes to mind was a lobbyist in Florida politics, doing well for himself. His wife's parents, devout Catholics, were celebrating their 50th anniversary, and they decided to go to Italy. During the planning, they made a bold request: They wanted to meet the Pope. That's obviously a tall order, one I did try to make happen, but it didn't come through.

Still, I wanted to do something meaningful for them. Without telling them, I arranged for a papal proclamation to commemorate their 50th anniversary. This wasn't something you could just buy online; there's no simple Vatican order form for it. I had to go to their church, get a signed letter from their priest confirming their faith and standing in the Catholic community, and send it off for approval. Eventually, a hand-painted scroll, created and delivered by the Vatican, arrived at their home about a month after their trip.

I didn't charge them anything. I didn't tell them I was doing it. It was never about business. It was about giving them an experience that money couldn't really buy – something special, sacred even, and deeply personal. It meant a lot to them, and honestly, it meant a lot to me too.

But why do it if I wasn't getting paid?

Well, because if someone did that for me, I'd never forget it. So why wouldn't I do it for them? That kind of gesture doesn't just come from obligation – it comes from understanding what's possible and choosing to act on it. So, when people ask, "Why invest so much in something you didn't get paid for?" I think the better question is: "Why wouldn't you?"

Most people don't do what they *can* do. Someone gives them rope, and they show you who they are. You don't get mad about it, you just take note. But sometimes, you *can* do something. And if you can, why not?

I used to keep a mental tab. "I did this for you, so something should come back to me." It was transactional, even if I didn't say it out loud. But somewhere along the way, I let that go.

One of the turning points came from my mom. She lent me money once, and I asked her how she wanted it repaid. She told me, "Look, if I get it back, great. If I don't, it's okay too. You should only ever lend money that way, never give more than you're okay with completely losing."

For example, years ago, a friend of mine was living in Colorado with his girlfriend, trying to build a life, but things were falling apart. One day, he called me. Said he was out of the apartment, living out of his car, no job, just the clothes on his back. I hung up the phone and immediately started calling everyone we knew. I pulled together enough money to get him gas and supplies so he could drive all the way back to Florida, because I knew once he got here, we could sort things out.

Fast-forward about fifteen years, and I found myself in a rough patch. I was struggling to make payroll, barely holding things together, and I needed help. I called him up and said, "Man, I just need grocery money."

"Done."

He didn't even hesitate.

You could say that's a transaction repaid. But it never felt like that. It wasn't a ledger we were keeping. It was just life.

You put good out into the universe and hope for the best. And sure, maybe it doesn't come back from the same place you gave it. But it *does* come back – sometimes in ways you least expect.

The Art of Asking Questions

Let me tell you what being rich really means.

Rich is when your son asks you to read him a story for the fifteenth time that day, and you say yes because you know someday he'll stop asking …

… Rich is when you can take an afternoon off to surprise your spouse with lunch, just because …

… Rich is having the mental space to notice that your friend seems off and actually asking them about it …

… Rich is being able to say "f*ck it" to the urgent and yes to the important.

So, reflecting on these questions, let's start to redefine rich:

1. **What does "being rich" mean to you right now?** Has that definition evolved over the years? Really think about it.

2. **Think of a time when life forced you to slow down, change course, or let go of control. Maybe it was an illness, a job loss, a breakup.**
   What emerged from that shift that surprised you? I'm betting something good came from it, even if you couldn't see it at the time.

3. **How many times have you convinced yourself something was "urgent" or "essential," only to realize later it didn't matter at all?**
What did that teach you? Those lessons are gold if you're willing to learn from them

4. **What is that "impossible" thing in your life right now? The one you've already decided can't happen. What if you allowed yourself to consider a different approach, a different perspective?**
What's really holding you back from that shift? Fear? Comfort? The opinion of others?

5. **What would it look like to invest more in a "return on intimacy" instead of a return on investment?**
How can you prioritize that starting today? Not next week. Not when things "calm down." Today.

PART II

The F*ck It Framework
Breaking Free
From Your Current

In life, we often find ourselves chasing a version of success that others have defined for us – one filled with external markers like money, status, and possessions. We build different versions of ourselves to fit into these expectations: the professional version, the family version, the social media version, and so on. But no matter how many versions we create, how many roles we play, or how many boxes we check off, the question remains: Are we truly living? Or are we simply surviving, fitting into molds that don't reflect who we really are?

The truth is, it's easy to get lost in the shuffle. Many of us hustle through life without pausing to ask ourselves the critical question: *What do I actually want?* And we find that the more we get, the emptier we feel. I've been there – a career that looked good on paper but felt hollow in practice, a life marked by accomplishments but lacking meaning. The more I ticked off the "success" checklist, the more disconnected I felt from myself.

That's when I had to face the truth: None of it mattered if it didn't align with who I truly was. If I wanted to live a life that felt real and full, I had to stop pretending. I had to stop fitting myself into molds that didn't serve me, and instead, break free from the expectations that were holding me back.

So if you're tired of living a life that doesn't fully reflect who you are or doesn't make you feel alive, then this chapter is for you. It's time to stop pretending, to stop hustling for things that don't matter, and to start living a life that's truly yours. And it starts with one simple, but radical decision: to say "F*ck it" to the versions of yourself you've been carrying and embrace the truth of who you really are.

Let's get started.

Chapter Four
Busy is Bullsh*t

"Beware the barrenness of a busy life."

– Socrates

We're all busy. In fact, we're all *too* busy. We're constantly chasing that next thing, forgetting about the little things that truly matter. Like the title of this chapter says, "busy is bullsh*t."

Nowadays, I don't even use the word anymore. It's lazy and doesn't really describe anything meaningful. You can still be "busy," but you can also express it in a more complete way. For example: "I've been working on this big project, and I'm excited to see how it will turn out," or "I've been taking some time to dive into a new book about a subject that is meaningful to me." That's a much more specific way of communicating, opposed to just dismissing someone with a vague "I'm busy." Merely saying you're busy is just an indistinct and fuzzy statement that doesn't convey much.

Think about it. Imagine you call up a friend and ask, "Hey, how you been doing?"

- Answer #1: "Oh, man, I've been super busy."

- Answer #2: "Actually, a lot has been going on. I was at an event this weekend for my business and made some amazing contacts. It was great to talk to some really like-minded people and get some new ideas on where I can take things, and then I also met this guy who wanted to partner with me."

Both are answers, yes, but which one do you prefer? Which one opens up communication and connection? It's not just about saying you're busy; it's about choosing to communicate clearly and meaningfully. Sure, saying you're busy is easy, but it doesn't say much, and it requires little effort. Plus, you're risking leaving out details that could spark interest, or worse, you might have to engage in conversations you don't feel like having.

Personally, I've been an open book for a long time. I don't have many secrets – maybe none at all. For instance, I've been arrested before. I've broken several laws, but none of them were ethically wrong. I once got arrested for felony drug possession, having four and a half pills of ecstasy on me. I was lucky to get away scot-free.

But here's the thing: I'd rather take a chance on opening up than hide behind that "busy" shield. Busy is quick and easy, and it gives people a chance to hide. A lot of people hide who they are, or they don't share what they're doing because they think it's uninteresting or that no one cares.

Too many of us are performing life instead of participating in it. We craft our image, tweak our LinkedIn bios, curate our Instagram feeds, and in the process, we stop actually being anything. We're "busy" doing things that look good on the outside, but don't feel good on the inside.

This is the trade-off: Performing is safe. Participating is vulnerable. When you show up fully, people can see you – and that means they can reject you. But it also means they can connect with you. You can't have the real rewards of life – real love, real friendship, real impact – without showing up as the real you.

If you want to start living a fuller life, you need to stop asking, "How will this make me look?" and start asking, "How will this make me feel?"

This is one thing I've learned from traveling and meeting people: People are all the same. We are all living life – surviving and filling that time when we're not surviving with the things we enjoy. We're not necessarily living our lives to the fullest yet, but there are very few out there hatching Machiavellian schemes to scam others. Now, I've met a few, but they're not the majority. And there are always clues. If you're paying attention, you can spot when something's off with someone.

When I joined Board of Advisors (BA) in 2018, I remember Mike Calhoun saying, "Everyone gets one hot seat. That's it."

But then one guy started getting multiple speaking spots. He was doing panels, giving talks, and showing up everywhere. And I thought, *Who is this guy?* He claimed to be ex-military Special Forces, now running an internet marketing company with a budget of a million dollars a month in Facebook ads for their clients.

I needed help with marketing, so I kept an open mind. I was ready to give up 20% of my company in exchange for a partnership with someone who could help with marketing, especially if they'd put up some of their own money for the ads. We started working on a deal, and this guy suggested I use his lawyer. I got a contract from his lawyer, and it was a mess of spelling errors and shoddy phrasing. Something was off. Then, he told me he was going to London for business, and I started suggesting all of these things he could do.

However, he stopped me. Budget was an issue. I wasn't suggesting extravagant things, at least not for the type of money he claimed he was making. A $250 dinner budget shouldn't have been a problem, right? *How can someone running a million dollars in ads have a problem with a $250 dinner?* That was a red flag.

I kept giving him rope, but I'm the type to take things slow, make sure everything's done properly. I prefer to really get to know people before jumping into business with them. And as it turns out, Jeremy Knauff, who runs a PR company in Tampa and was also U.S. Marine, did some digging.

We found out that this guy wasn't Special Forces at all – he was actually in supply, not a military operator. He'd been scamming people, running a Ponzi scheme within the BA community, and defrauding millions.

I dodged a bullet there. It taught me that taking things slow is sometimes the best approach. This guy and I parted ways because, as he put it, "I like to move fast," but I wasn't attached to the outcome. People often react out of the fear of missing out, but that's no way to live. Taking your time, being patient, and making sure things are legit will always serve you better than rushing into something because you're scared of losing out.

Chasing Who We Are

Most people never ask themselves the real questions – not because they don't care, but because they're scared of the answers. Who am I, really? What do I actually want? These are not convenient questions. They disrupt things. They shine lights on places we'd rather keep dark – relationships that don't fit, jobs that drain us, stories we inherited but never questioned.

The truth is that not asking those questions doesn't keep the discomfort away, it just delays it. Eventually, life forces your hand. A breakup, a health scare, a moment when the mask slips and you realize the role you've been playing doesn't fit anymore. The sooner you start asking, the sooner you can start living a life that feels like yours – not someone else's idea of who you should be.

Personally, I've always been a "f*ck it" kind of person, wildly chasing who I am for decades, ever since I was around seventeen.

My dad had what you might call a stereotypical Irish temper. One of my earliest memories is actually a good one – at least, it started that way. We were on a beach in West Palm. I was a curious kid, asking him a bunch of ridiculous questions like how many grains of sand were on the beach or how far we were from the sun. Dumb stuff, sure, but the kind of wonder kids live on.

His response was to get upset. He kicked me in the gut, knocked the wind right out of me, and just walked off. Conversation over.

That set a tone.

Later, when I was maybe twelve or thirteen, I came home from a friend's house to a water balloon fight happening out front. Within minutes, I was filling balloons in the garage when one of the neighbor kids snuck up, launched a balloon at me, missed, and it slammed against the washing machine. Loud as hell. My dad heard the noise, stormed out, and saw me standing right there at the sink. What I didn't know was that my aunt had dropped off her baby, who was napping, and my dad was on edge about the house staying quiet. The baby didn't wake up, but none of that mattered. When I mouthed off, confused and defensive, he went red-hot furious. He chased me out back, caught me, and bent me backward with his hand on my neck.

That was the bridge too far. For me, and probably for him too. I ran straight to the neighbor's house and called the cops. Had him arrested. Between me and my brother, I was the one who stood up and said, "F*ck that. It's over."

The charges were dropped under a deal with the DA: If he ever touched me again, the old charges would come roaring back with the new ones. It was the first time he couldn't touch me, couldn't control me.

I didn't have physical power over him, but I had real power for the first time.

Of course, there were costs. His parents, my grandparents, cut me off completely. If they called and I answered the phone, they'd just hang up. I never spoke to my grandfather again before he died. But the funny thing is, my dad and I probably only have a relationship today because I did what I did. About two years later, my dad apologized. We are not best friends, but I've enjoyed seeing him develop a genuine relationship with Corsten; it shows me just how much he has changed and grown. I respect him for who he is and who he's become, and together, we have certainly come a long way from those days.

Growing up, I was pretty much feral. My mom and dad were both workaholics who were gone most of the time, so after school, I did whatever I wanted. Bike rides, basketball, TV marathons, whatever. Nobody really cared. It was total freedom without direction.

The first real break from everything came when I was an exchange student in Barcelona before my senior year of high school. For the first time, I had real separation from any authority figure. After classes ended, I didn't have to take the extra English classes the other students did, which left me with hours to myself every day. I'd pull out the subway map, close my eyes, point to a spot, and go. No plan, just explore.

At first, I barely spoke Spanish, but after a few months of wandering the city alone, I got good enough that people were shocked when the American kid with baggy jeans opened his mouth and spoke in Spanish, not English. Those months were huge. I spent hours just by myself. No distractions, no safety nets. It forced me to start asking uncomfortable questions: "Who am I?" "What do I actually believe?"

It's messy at first. When you start asking those questions, you're bad at it. But if you stick with it, the answers start showing up.

When I turned eighteen, the questioning deepened. I had been raised Lutheran, but I started wondering: *Am I Lutheran?* I realized I didn't know anything about other religions. So I started reading anything I could find. Buddhism, especially the philosophy behind it, spoke to me far more than anything I'd been taught growing up, and eventually, all that searching led to my first tattoo: an OM symbol, modified with a Ganesh head.

I liked that fusion of Hindu and Tibetan Buddhist ideas, different views of the same mystery. Also, the elephant is tied back to my college, whose mascot is an elephant. Everything had to mean something. I spent ten years thinking about getting that tattoo. When I finally did, I didn't want it hidden. I wanted it where I could see it every day, a reminder of everything I'd been through and everything I still was.

Most of my twenties were an extended experiment in asking, "Who am I?" Relationships, jobs, beliefs, even appearances. I pierced my tongue. Dyed my hair all sorts of colors. Grew it long, chopped it short. Skydived. Indoor skydived. Rollerbladed at fifty miles an hour. Crawled out of a moving car's moonroof at seventy. Chased adrenaline, chased experiences, chased every possible version of myself until I could say, "Nope, not that one."

But I never felt I was running from something; I was running toward something, even if I didn't know exactly what. I was figuring it out the only way I knew how: living it, asking the questions, making mistakes, and not letting fear shut me down.

A lot of people get stuck waiting for clarity before they act. They think they need a blueprint. They don't. You didn't need one either. You figured it out the way most of us actually do: through motion. You tried things. You got it wrong. You didn't wait for certainty; you built confidence by doing.

Chasing who you are isn't a straight line. It's messy, weird, and often embarrassing. But not chasing it – that's the real danger. That's how you end up stuck in a life you resent, playing a role you never auditioned for. If there's one message in this chapter, it's this: You don't need a perfect plan. You just need the guts to move.

You'll Never Win
the Busy Olympics

"Don't confuse movement with progress.
Because you can run in place
and not get anywhere."

– Denzel Washington

The hamster wheel we're all stuck on isn't broken, it's just not meant to go anywhere. Think about it: You get a job so you can make money, buy a house, buy a car, and feed your family. You hit those goals, and for a little while, it feels great. But then, somehow, it's not enough anymore. So you chase another job, maybe get a 15% or 20% raise, so you can make more money – to pay for the house, to pay for the car, to feed the family. Then that doesn't feel like enough, either. You get headhunted, switch jobs again, make even more money … And the cycle continues.

All the while, if you had just stayed put, you probably could have paid off the first house. But instead, you refinanced it or sold it and bought a bigger house. It's a never-ending loop: Work harder, make more, spend more, *need* more. And it's not just homes or cars. It's the whole culture – fast fashion, fast furniture, fast food, fast tech … None of it's built to last.

Everything is meant to be temporary, to get you to spend again and again, which forces you to run even faster on the wheel.

One of the great lies we're sold is that "more" will fix things. More money, more status, more stuff. But "more" doesn't automatically lead to better. In fact, it often just means more responsibility, more pressure, more noise. When you chase the next promotion or a bigger house thinking it will make you happier, you're usually just moving the goalpost.

The real antidote to this isn't scaling back everything – it's consciously choosing what matters. If you don't choose, the culture will choose for you. And it will always choose more. But when you learn to say, "This is enough," you reclaim power. And with that power, you can start designing a life around purpose, not pressure – with that power, you start to build generational wealth.

One of the greatest things that real generational wealth does is break the cycle. True wealth – the kind that's passed down – often looks like a house that's already paid for, furniture that's actually built to last, assets that don't have to be replaced every few years. These things seem small, but they give the next generation an incredible gift: They don't have to work just to survive. They can choose to work on what they *want* to do. That choice to work from purpose instead of desperation is the real definition of freedom.

But it comes with responsibility – on both sides.

One generation needs to set the foundation, but the next generation has to be invested enough to appreciate what they were given. They must become good stewards of what was handed down, and not just survive, but *thrive* and build upon it for the generation after them – at a higher level than before.

Without that stewardship, even the greatest fortunes evaporate.

I used to run a genealogy package, teaming up with a Peabody Award-winning documentarian and an ex-CIA researcher. If you had the budget, we would trace your family's roots as far back as possible, then design a trip for you and your family to visit those origins. We'd capture the whole journey on film, telling the story of how your ancestors tended potato fields, braved impossible odds, built businesses, and clawed their way to better lives.

We did this because of a staggering statistic: If you fast-forward three generations, 92% of all fortunes, no matter how big, are gone. Why? Because later generations often have no understanding of what it took to get there. They have no idea of the struggle, the sacrifices, the grit that built that fortune. So when millions or billions fall into their laps, they often spend it searching for meaning, and too often, in the absence of meaning, they turn to distraction. Drugs, endless parties, waste. Without purpose, destruction follows.

The point of our work was to show generations of work and sacrifice. Here's what it took to get here, here's what it takes to keep it, and here's what you can build from it. That's what it means to build a legacy.

So, ask yourself: What legacy are you creating right now, even if you never use the word? Is it one of exhaustion and endless striving? Or one of presence, clarity, and intention?

Because you don't win the Busy Olympics. You just burn out in public. And the prize? Emptiness.

The Art of Asking Questions

You become who you are by trying, failing, risking, reflecting. By being in motion. You don't need a perfect plan. You need courage. The courage to slow down. The courage to ask better questions. The courage to choose meaning over momentum.

Ask yourself the following reflection questions:

1. **If you stopped chasing "more," what would "enough" look like for you – and how would your daily life need to change to align with that?**
   What would a life less focused on progress look like? Think about how redefining "enough" might allow you to build a life rooted in intention.

2. **When was the last time you said, "I'm busy"? What were you really avoiding – connection, discomfort, vulnerability, or clarity?**
   Reflect on the purpose that response served. Was it honest or convenient? How often do you use the word "busy" as an excuse, and what is it really masking in your life?

3. **How much do you value personal growth and self-discovery, and in what ways have you "experimented" with who you are?**

How can you push yourself beyond your perceived comfort zones?

4. **Do you tend to rush into decisions out of fear, or do you take the time to evaluate things thoroughly and trust your instincts?**
   How can you slow down and trust yourself more in decision-making?

5. **How can you start to integrate more authenticity and openness into your daily communication, both in personal relationships and in your professional life?**
   What would that shift look like for you? Honestly, ask yourself, who you are and also who you want to be.

We wear "busy" like armor. It deflects curiosity, connection, and, most importantly, accountability. It gives us something to hide behind when we don't want to be seen. But real growth starts when we take that armor off and choose to show up, flawed and figuring it out.

So, one more question: Are you ready to take that armor off?

Chapter Five
The Search for Meaning (In a World Obsessed with Metrics)

"Not everything that can be counted counts, and not everything that counts can be counted."

– William Bruce Cameron

Sometimes I find myself doom-scrolling for an hour. I see all of the news and start wondering where humanity is really heading. With so much instability and the threat of AI and robots rapidly taking over more and more jobs, I can't help but ask: Are people going to be psychologically able to handle it? What does it even mean to be human if you don't have to work anymore?

Think about it. Imagine you're someone who builds cars. Not a custom maker or an artisan, but a worker on the Ford assembly line. You put tires on cars all day long. Then one day, that job disappears because a machine can do it faster and cheaper. Suddenly, your purpose is gone. Your routine, your role in the world, is wiped out. And you're left asking yourself: "Who am I without my job?"

This is something we do all the time; we define ourselves by what we do rather than who we are. I am an attorney. I am a cashier. I am a teacher. I am this. I am that. We stamp ourselves with a label without even thinking. It's automatic. But those titles, as familiar as they are, don't actually capture anything about who we really are. They don't even touch the essence of our humanity.

Instead, it feels like we're constantly chasing after the next distraction – the next promotion, the next project, the next "thing" – because stopping long enough to sit with that bigger question is uncomfortable.

So, who are you, *really*? Do you even need to have a contribution? Isn't just *being you* enough? Are you a human *being* or a human *doing*?

Most people don't know that it is. But the real challenge is finding that answer for yourself, not for anyone else. It's deeply personal. No one can hand it to you.

We've been taught from the moment we were born that we must be productive members of society, or, if not, to be constantly distracted. Always doing. Always consuming. Rarely just *being*.

For the first time, at least consciously, I gave myself some real space the other day. I was driving, and normally I'm a windows-down, radio-up kind of guy. I love music – old-school rap, EDM, classic rock, alt. rock – honestly, pretty much everything except country. Usually, I crank it up and lose myself in it. But this time, my mind was racing even with the music blaring, and I realized it wasn't helping.

So I did something different. I turned the radio off. I kept the windows down. I slowed down the car and started taking some side roads. I let the tires rumble over them, felt the vibration, listened to the sound of the wheels, the birds, the wind. I drove around Lake Hollingsworth, a place a lot of people walk or jog around, and as I cruised past at twenty, twenty-five miles an hour, I caught tiny snippets of conversation drifting out into the evening air. It was this completely visceral experience, this quiet awareness.

No chasing thrills. No flooring it for the rush. No blasting songs for the hit of dopamine. Just being in the moment.

Suddenly, I realized just how many of these kinds of moments we miss because we don't create space for them. Maybe it only meant as much as it did because of everything I'm going through now, maybe it's the diagnosis, maybe it's just getting older, but it hit me hard.

Time isn't necessarily running out faster than it was before.

But the quality of that time? That's what feels different. That's what feels urgent.

Realistically, there's a decent chance I could live a long time despite my diagnosis – my family has longevity in our blood. My dad's father lived to 70, my mom's father sadly died in a car wreck in his 60s, my dad's mother lived to 96, and my mom's mother is still alive at 95, and ... So, if I'm lucky, I could live to 80, maybe more. But living isn't the same as *being alive*. The question isn't just how long I have. It's whether I'll have control over my body. Whether I'll remember my wife, my child. Whether I'll still feel like *me*. That's what matters – the difference between being technically alive and *truly living*.

And so now, I see distraction everywhere. It's in the fabric of everything.

Who doesn't love spending a few minutes scrolling Instagram or Reddit or TikTok? Hey, I even mentioned it as something I do at the beginning of this chapter. The algorithm is so good now. It knows what we love, what we might love, and what will get us fired up. It serves everything up like butter; it's designed to distract us, and it works.

But what do we have to show for it afterward? Maybe a few good laughs to share with friends. Maybe some cool memes. That's not nothing – I genuinely admire some of the creativity people have. I don't hate it. But I also recognize the cost it takes. It's not just about what you're seeing anymore. It's about what's being hidden from you, behind the curtain. It's what you're *not* noticing while you're laughing at that clip or liking that photo.

This is why being intentional matters. What you do with your time. Where you spend your attention. Who you invest in.

How many people do you know who actually think about *who they are* anymore? How many people truly nurture their close friendships, stay connected on purpose, instead of letting the calendar slide by?

I can't even count how many times I've run into someone and the first thing they say is, "Man, I've just been so busy." It's automatic. A reflex. But lately, I'm trying really hard not to say I'm "busy" anymore. Sure, I have a lot of things to do. But "busy" isn't a badge of honor – remember, busy is bullsh*t. It just means you're letting life happen to you instead of living it on purpose.

Noticing the Unnoticed

If you're not looking for it, you won't see it. That's just the truth.

I remember when I first got out of college, I went to work for Ford Motor Credit. I was part of an experimental class, something they had never done before, and honestly, I don't know if they ever did it again. Up to that point, they had been promoting credit analysts from within their collections department. But they started realizing that people who came up through collections were less likely to approve riskier loans, what we called C and D paper.

In case you're not familiar with the term, "C and D paper" refers to loan applicants with lower credit scores. A-paper borrowers, the gold standard, are people with credit scores around 800; they're a lock, virtually guaranteed to pay you back. B-paper borrowers are still solid – maybe somewhere between 680 and 700 – and while life events could throw them off track, they're generally reliable bets. Then you get into C paper, around the 640 mark, and D paper, which is anything lower.

It's kind of like letter grades in school. The thing is A-paper makes Ford almost no money; it's practically a pass-through rate from the banks. Maybe they eke out a tiny profit. B-paper is a little better, maybe a point or two of interest margin. But C and D paper? That's where the real profit lives, and back then, you were talking about 12% to 14% interest rates. Those high-interest loans subsidized the safer ones.

At the time, Ford realized their credit processing wasn't profitable enough, so they decided to try hiring analysts straight out of college … People just like me. They flew about a hundred of us up to Detroit for interviews that lasted three days. They put us in a hotel, wined and dined us like we were royalty, and even gave us a private dinner inside the closed Henry Ford Museum. They had eight of the best chefs in town preparing food, and you could just wander, eat, drink, and even tour the exhibits after hours. They paired each of us up with executives who, they assured us, were *not* involved in the hiring decisions, but I wasn't naive enough to believe they didn't have some influence. They took us to the Ford test track too, and we got to drive everything Ford owned, from F-150 Lightnings to Jaguars.

It was serious headhunting. At the end, you were either hired or you weren't. I got the job, along with about 80 others in that initial batch, and another 60 or 70 people came in the next class. The plan was to have massive growth.

But then real life happened.

While I was in Detroit for training, 9/11 occurred. On top of that, there was the whole Firestone tire debacle with the Ford Explorers flipping over. It was just a mess. Ford had projected business growth, but instead, they had to start contracting. I was placed at the Dallas-Fort Worth office, the second busiest outside of Detroit itself, and it was intense.

I personally handled between 500 and 700 million dollars of Ford's money every year, and would usually go through about 120 credit applications before 10 AM. It was no joke.

Eventually, Ford had to downsize, and I got laid off. Honestly, it worked out fine for me. I found a job at a Hyundai-Buick dealership in Jacksonville, Florida.

At the time, I didn't even know Buicks were a thing. Like, how many Buicks could they possibly sell? I barely even noticed them on the road. Then, on the drive from Texas to Jacksonville, I saw them. Buicks. Everywhere. One after another. It was like I had tuned into some hidden frequency that had been there all along. That's when I realized: Buicks are the brand that just melts into the background. They aren't flashy or bold. They're dependable, sure, but not stylish or exciting. They're "luxury-lite" – slightly better than a Chevy, not quite a Cadillac. In other words, the world's *okayest* car. Yet tons of people bought them; I just never saw it until I was looking.

And that's the real point. You won't see what you're not looking for. If you aren't looking for meaning in your life, you won't find it. If you're not seeking out good relationships, you'll never build them. If you aren't actively trying to be a good parent or spouse, those opportunities will pass you by without you even realizing it.

So right now, I want you to do this:

Choose one daily habit you normally fill with noise – scrolling during lunch, watching something before bed, turning on music during your commute. Just once, remove the distraction and do it in full presence.

Ask yourself:
- What do I notice that I usually miss?
- How does my body feel when it's not being fed constant input?
- What thoughts float up when I stop running from silence?

You might be surprised what surfaces. It won't all be pretty – but it will be real.

There's a saying that what you focus on multiplies, and it's absolutely true. Whether you're intentional or not, your attention will land somewhere. So if you're going to focus on something anyway, why not choose wisely? Make it something good. Otherwise, you'll wake up 30 or 40 years later with little to show for it – maybe a lot of funny memes, but not much real substance. Sure, you'll remember sending that GIF of Homer Simpson disappearing into the bushes after someone ghosted you for a few days. That's a great little moment. It's fun, like salt on a good meal. But if all you eat is salt, you're headed for high blood pressure and a lot worse.

Life needs more than seasoning. It needs something solid underneath.

The AI Replacement…
I Don't Think So

Rightfully so, a lot of people are worried about AI. It has incredible potential to outperform us in nearly every aspect, and while it is currently confined to our computers, laptops, and phones, there is no reason to believe that in the next 5–10 years we won't have independently mobile robots running on the same software. But that being said, I think there is something we have that AI will never truly have.

"Beingness."

We are human *beings*, and as human beings, we get to experience this world in our own unique way. Each one of us has our own perspective, our own opinion, and that means that the world is entirely different for each of us. AI is trained from lines of code and data. The exact same thing over and over again to get the "best" result. But being human, experiencing life to the fullest, is not about getting the "best" result – it's about the messy journey we take to get to the result we want.

For example, can AI do what I do? Absolutely not. Not a chance in hell. And I feel confident saying that.

AI might be able to give you suggestions on where to go for a holiday, but at the end of the day, it's not different from looking at a brochure. It doesn't take away the stress, it doesn't customize the experience; it gives you the "best" result for what you've asked, and then you have to go out and do the extra legwork. So, do I feel comfortable that I have a job going into the next few years? Yeah, I do.

Because the truth is, I'm doing things AI simply can't. I think about the experience. I use personal connections that aren't available to any machine. I create opportunities while coordinating a hundred moving parts, across different timeframes and variables, most of which AI can't even recognize. It doesn't know when a client's about to smile, or why they're about to smile. But I do.

Most of my clients don't directly ask me for all this complexity. They don't always know what's possible. But I understand what moments they'll have, and I plan them months in advance. I know exactly when a smile's going to cross their face, and I know why it's going to happen.

One of our clients recently took a canal cruise in Belgium, which we organized for them. Anyone else, or AI, would have told her to hop on a train or hire a driver. Thirty minutes, no big deal, point A to B and you're in the next town, easy. Instead, I repositioned a boat three and a half hours that morning, from Ghent to Bruges, just to pick them up. Then three and a half hours back down, cruising all the way.

Why? Because I knew the canal ran right up to the hotel where they were checking in. I knew the experience of pulling up by boat would be unforgettable. They didn't just travel from Ghent to Bruges; they *experienced* Belgium. They floated through small towns, farms, and historic homes along the water. They saw the whole country from a perspective that no train window could give them.

And because a three-and-a-half-hour boat ride is cool in itself, I went further: champagne, great local beers, and a full charcuterie spread onboard. Even better, the two guys piloting the boat were from Ghent themselves, giving them an impromptu local's guide to everything they were seeing. One of the captains even came from a family that had been boatmen for over 100 years. That's the difference.

AI will get you there, sure. It'll find your hotel, and recommend a few "top 10" lists. But it's just a faster version of planning your own trip. If you want complexity, nuance, connection, then you go to a real person, because it can't do that. For me, as a professional, I can send a two-line email and ensure you get a truly incredible experience rather than a "top 10" experience.

You really want to make sure you're going to the *right* people. Lots of travel agents today bank on partnerships like Virtuoso or Signature – they pay to be part of those networks, and they can offer their clients little perks like a free bottle of champagne because of their membership contracts.

But I'm not a Virtuoso or Signature agent. On purpose. I don't want their contracts. If you pay me for an Italian vacation, and you check into your hotel and find a bottle of French champagne, I've just diluted the experience you hired me to create. I'm here to build something authentic, something locally immersive, not just drop the same luxury perks all over the world, regardless of where you are.

See, what I realized is none of my clients are experts in the local specialties of the places they're visiting. Have you ever heard of a *calisson*? How about a *couque de Dinant*? Probably not. A *calisson* is a little almond-flavored, sugar-coated candy from Provence. A *couque de Dinant* is a super hard honey-based cookie from Belgium. You don't stumble on those easily. They're sold in street stalls, wrapped in paper bags, hidden in tiny towns where no guidebook tells you to go.

If you're wandering around Provence and you see a *calisson* in a shop, you might buy one, or you might not. You probably won't know what it is. You might pass right by. And if you do buy one, you'll most likely try it once, good or bad, and never realize if you tasted the best or just an okay version. That's how most people experience local specialties: by accident, without context, without the story that gives them meaning.

Scenario two is worse: Now you know what a *calisson* is because I told you. You're in Provence. How many stores do you think you'll visit trying to find the very best one? One? Maybe two if you're super curious? Most people will try once, and that's it. Whether you got the best or the worst, you won't know. It's hit or miss.

My clients hire me to be an expert in the places they're traveling. So I built a program where we identify the best locally sourced, locally produced specialty in every area we do business – and we have one delivered straight to their room every single day.

It could be candy, it could be artisan knives, jewelry, handmade perfumes, clothing, pottery … It doesn't matter what the item is, it matters that it's authentic, it's local, and it's not something you can buy in a tourist trap. Each one comes with a sense of place that the algorithm can't replicate.

The Art of Asking Questions

Meaning isn't handed to you; it's revealed slowly, through reflection, discomfort, and small moments of awareness. Sit in the moment now and ask yourself:

1. **Do you define yourself by what you do, and how can you start focusing on who you are beyond titles and labels?**
    What aspects of yourself are you overlooking in your pursuit of success or recognition?

2. **What does "truly living" mean to you?**
    How can you begin to embody that definition more fully in your day-to-day life?

3. **How do you respond when you lose a sense of purpose, and what steps can you take to reconnect with yourself when that happens?**
    What can you do to prevent losing your sense of purpose in the first place?

4. **How can you shift your focus from chasing external measures of success to focusing on cultivating more authentic, meaningful experiences and connections?**
    What would this shift look like in practice? What would it do for the people around you?

5. **What's one thing you can do today to *be* more, and *do* less – intentionally?**

   Remember, legacy isn't about the end – it's about your choices now.

In a world that worships productivity and metrics, there's a quiet revolution waiting to be discovered – one that starts inside each of us. Let this be an invitation – not to solve your life in one sitting, but to pause, just long enough to hear the quieter voice inside. Because that's where the good stuff is.

Chapter Six
The River Doesn't Resist

"The only thing guaranteed
to never change is that everything
is always changing."

– Louis L'Amour

The more you try to grasp onto something, the more it slips through your fingers. You can't hold onto time, or a single moment, or any situation. Everything is like sand slipping through your hands. But what the majority of us do is try to grab it. We try to control our circumstances and hold onto specific moments, forgetting that life is constantly changing.

Time flows like a river, and you can either fight against it or you can learn to navigate the currents. Life isn't about trying to freeze a moment in time – it's about learning how to let go and ride the waves of change. When we let go of the need for control, we create space for spontaneity, creativity, and growth.

So, over the course of the next week, intentionally identify one area of your life where you are gripping too tightly.

It could be a routine, a relationship, or even your expectations for yourself. Each time you feel the urge to control, ask yourself: "What would happen if I let go?"

Then, take one small action to release that grip. It could be allowing a conversation to unfold without interference, letting a situation resolve without your input, or trusting that things will work out without your constant planning.

At the end of the week, reflect on how it felt to embrace uncertainty and allow life to unfold naturally. Did you feel more at peace? More energized? Or did you feel like you made a "bad decision"?

We often see "bad decisions" as something to be avoided at all costs. But sometimes, those "bad decisions" are exactly what we need to let loose, have fun, and remind ourselves that not everything has to be serious. Life isn't just about calculating risks and avoiding mistakes – it's about enjoying the moments of spontaneity and embracing the lessons that come with the unpredictability.

Full disclosure: I've had my moments of throwing caution to the wind, of making bad decisions, and of partying too hard. I've lived through it. For example, when we were in Philadelphia, the hotel gave us poker chips for free sangria at the bar. I loved sangria, so I had seven poker chips – one for each night of our stay. I used two one night, and then I had five left for the final evening.

I asked Christina if she wanted a drink, but she wasn't into wine, so I went to the bar by myself. I told the bartender, "I'm here to make some bad decisions." I ordered five sangrias, and I asked him to give me a tray to carry them all. The bartender laughed and said, "Alright, let's see how this goes."

I took all five of those sangrias back to my room that night and had a great time.

The point is, sometimes it's okay to make "bad decisions" and embrace the unpredictability of life. Life is to be lived, so have some fun and let loose when the moment feels right.

Giving Rope

If people can sometimes live to 100 years old, we're only about 50 generations removed from the beginning of humanity. Isn't that crazy to think about? It's one of those things you don't really consider. When you break it down, we're essentially evolved monkeys. But the thing is, we're still evolving, even though so many of us don't realize it because we're stuck on that hamster wheel, caught in a cycle that keeps us moving but never really getting anywhere.

It's like the movie *The Matrix* – think about all the people who weren't unplugged. They don't want to be. They're comfortable with the stresses they have and the things they need to deal with. Even when things go wrong, at least it's familiar to them. The unfamiliar is scary to so many people. They'd rather stick with the known, even if it's not great, because at least it feels safe.

I think a lot of it comes from how I grew up. Every two to three years, I was in a new place, having to make new friends. That forced me to accept that nothing is permanent – you learn to embrace uncertainty. For me, uncertainty became okay, because I had to keep finding new people, new connections, new "tribes" to be a part of. Life isn't stable, and once you get used to that, you stop fearing change.

I had a friend who used to live here in town. He was the typical IT guy – introverted, geeky, and a little offbeat. He'd say some wacky stuff, and sometimes it was clear he needed guidance. So, I took him under my wing, taught him how to talk to girls, and showed him how to handle himself socially. He couldn't just go up to a waitress and say the kind of weird stuff he used to say. It wasn't working, and it wasn't funny. He had no idea how bad it came off, so I stepped in.

We were really good friends for a long time. But then, he moved to Dallas and started a new IT company. Years passed, and one day, he called me up. He said, "Let's hang out. I've got tickets to see Amy Schumer, and then we can grab dinner and drinks." I thought, *Sure, let's do it.* We ended up getting pretty drunk, and on our way out of the casino after the show, something strange happened.

I was in the car, and he was walking toward me holding a fire extinguisher he'd stolen from the garage. His idea was to bring it to my car as a funny prank. I cracked the window and said, "Bro, go put that back." He dropped it 10 feet away, but I told him, "You're not getting in my car until you put it back where you found it." Why? For one thing, fire safety – it's not something to mess around with. Second, we were in a casino parking lot, cameras everywhere, and they probably already had my tag. I didn't want to risk getting into any trouble for something that wasn't even funny.

He got incredibly pissed, stormed off, and took an Uber back to his hotel. We didn't speak for months after that. But that moment showed me who he really was. What is a friendship worth if someone is willing to put me and my family in jeopardy for some dumb prank? That was the turning point for me; it put a major dent in our relationship.

And that's when I came up with what I call the "giving rope" philosophy. When I meet someone new or enter a new relationship, I'm initially quiet. Myself, but watchful – I just blend in, hang back, and observe. I give people as much rope as they need. If you ask for my help or advice, I'm all in. But I also let people show me who they are. I believe that in the end, people will either prove themselves worthy of all that rope or they'll hang themselves with it. It's inevitable. One of those two things will happen, 100% of the time.

I've learned that everyone has a representative version of themselves, their "secretary," the person they want you to see. But I'm not interested in that. I want to see who you really are, your true self. Are you aware of what you do? Are you thoughtful? Are you the kind of person who just does whatever they want without considering the consequences? If that's you, that's fine, we can be friendly. But if you start putting a fire extinguisher in my car, we're going to have a problem.

So, how do you differentiate? Because, let's face it, everyone's going to do dumb things. We all have our unconscious moments in life. The key is figuring out when to draw the line between being friendly with someone and being true friends.

Sometimes people mess up, but that doesn't mean it's their character. I've had moments where someone's done something stupid, but it's clear it's not who they are at their core. We can move past it.

That friend who tried to do the dumb "prank" while drunk, well, after he deeply apologized. Turns out, a lot of his actions were influenced by some unhealthy stuff going on with his relationship. His girlfriend was throwing shade at me, thinking Christina was really into him. It was a whole drama in his head, and it took a while for him to work through it. I accepted his apology. But the truth is, before all that happened, if he had called me at 2 AM, I'd have answered right away, no questions asked. That's changed. Before, he was in my inner circle, someone I'd prioritize. Now? That's not the case anymore. We're still friends, but we're not *as* close as we were – and he has to be okay with that. Maybe someday, things will go back to where they were, but not today.

This is a big part of how life works: Nothing is permanent. We all do dumb stuff sometimes. I've done my share of things that needed forgiveness. But those moments don't define me, and they don't have to define anyone else either.

My wife Christina and I often talk about this because she sees the world through a lens where, to her, most people are good, thoughtful, and nice. On the other hand, I think most people are just unaware, not really paying attention to their actions or how they impact others. The funny thing is, when someone does something really stupid, she's let down. For me, though, I see it coming. I'm not surprised. But when someone does something truly amazing, it stands out. To me, that's noteworthy. She's just like, "Of course they did something great."

So, while she spends much of her time being let down, I get surprised when people rise above. That's the part I love – it's the best feeling when people exceed expectations. But it's important to realize that most people will let you down at some point. You have to accept that. And when someone doesn't, you should be incredibly grateful. The trick is not to feel slighted or jaded or disappointed when that disappointment happens.

Remember, we don't want to attach ourselves to the outcome.

It's okay if people aren't thinking about their lives from an outside perspective. I've been there myself. Life is full of phases, and everyone is going through something at any given time. I don't begrudge people for being idiots or making mistakes. I've been there. I know that whatever bad or indifferent phase they're in, it's going to change. Just like I've changed.

Diving Deeper Than the Surface

Someone once said, "I'd rather have four quarters than 99 pennies." This is often used to describe how we view relationships – we want to have a few good, meaningful relationships rather than countless disconnected acquaintances. However, it works for every other area of our lives as well. The idea is that they would want to have fewer things of higher value in their life, rather than more things of less value. We are always chasing more, stuck running on the hamster wheel in the attempt to find the next bigger and better thing to fill our lives. It's how I lived my life for the longest time.

See, I didn't know what I liked or wanted. So I tried *everything.* Well, maybe not *everything* everything, but enough to know I was casting an extremely wide net. I approached every area of my life, every opportunity and experience with the attitude of "I don't know if I'll like this, but I'll find out." And so I played piano (couldn't really play). Tried basketball (wasn't very good). Jumped into dozens of things where I was okay, decent even, but never great. Never *excellent.* And it took me a long time to realize what that meant.

When I heard that metaphor, "I'd rather have four quarters than 99 pennies," I realized I was living a life full of surfaces: surface skills, surface interests, surface conversations, surface connections … Nothing really went as deep as it could, or should have.

Yet, when we realize that, we still don't go deep because we're scared of being uncomfortable – we're scared of conflict. Real depth requires conflict … disagreement, vulnerability, discomfort, hardship, challenge … You have to ask hard questions. You have to draw lines – about who you are, what you believe – and be willing to let someone else do the same. But most people never go there.

You can spend *years* around someone and still not know who they really are – or let them see who you are – because we never go beyond the surface. And it's not that those relationships are bad. They're fun, they're friendly, but they're not your *tribe*. They're not the people who fill your soul.

Before I met Christina, I was constantly on the move – the kind of person who was either at someone's house or hosting people at mine five nights a week. I was rarely alone. Whether it was dating, catching up with friends, heading to a bar, or bouncing from one social plan to the next, I was always in motion. You could've called me a surface-level social butterfly, flitting from one interaction to another, soaking in the noise, the motion, the company. That kind of lifestyle felt normal to me – probably a side effect of ADHD. There was always someone to see, somewhere to be, and I loved being invited everywhere.

But something shifted.

Over time, I stopped saying yes to every invite. Not because I didn't care, but because the scenes started to feel hollow. These days, I don't get as many invitations – not because the people disappeared, but because I consciously stepped back. A lot of the people I once ran with are still doing their thing – the same kind of parties, the same kind of crowds. They'll throw a Super Bowl party or something for the Masters, or maybe a random weekend bash with 75 or 100 people packed into a house. The kind of gatherings where you have to shout over the music and the buzz of conversation just to ask the same few recycled questions: "What do you do?" "Where are you from?" "How long have you lived around here?" Then rinse and repeat with the next person.

Eventually, I realized I can't do that anymore.

It's not that I've become antisocial, or that I think I'm above any of it. Honestly, a part of me still finds moments of fun in those settings. But I've learned to recognize that they just don't fill my cup. They don't leave me feeling seen, heard, or connected in any real way. They leave me drained. Empty.

These days, I'd much rather spend time with my wife Christina and maybe one or two other couples. That's the kind of night that lights me up – one where we actually connect, where we laugh deep belly laughs, share stories, ask questions that matter, and feel like we're truly in each other's lives.

We can talk about the real stuff – not just the surface gloss. We can get into it. And that's what I've come to value more than anything else.

And the same is true for interests.

I'm into *everything*: politics, science, engineering, architecture, cars, finance, real estate, psychology, design ... I've read whitepapers I barely understood just to chase curiosity. But I have limited time, limited energy. So I had to start saying "No," even to things I genuinely liked, so I could say a more powerful "Yes" to the few things that really matter.

One of the most important things I've learned, maybe more than anything else, is to build a few simple, flexible rules for myself. Not strict, hyper-specific commandments, but broad principles that guide my choices in a variety of situations. This is where I think a lot of people go wrong: They make a mistake, then try to correct it with an extremely specific rule. Something like, "I'll never text my ex after midnight again," or "I won't check my phone during meetings." Sure, these rules are born out of experience, but each one only applies to one narrow moment.

When you live like that, you end up with a rulebook that's 100 pages long. And guess what? No human being is wired to remember and apply 100 individual rules every day. It becomes impossible to follow.

You've built a system that's designed to collapse, and when it does, it leads to constant disappointment. In Buddhism, they call this *dukkha* – suffering. Not just the external kind, but the internal friction that comes from repeatedly failing yourself. You break your own rules, then you beat yourself up, then you make more rules. It's a cycle of self-imposed punishment.

So I've chosen a different route: I make fewer rules, and I make them broad. I try to keep it to five or fewer. That way, they're memorable. They're flexible. They apply to more than one situation, which makes them useful on a daily basis. You avoid most of the common traps and don't have to mentally flip through a giant list of dos and don'ts. They become automatic, internalized.

The best rules are like a Christmas tree – one trunk, but a lot of branches. You don't need 100 little trees or a single, flimsy branch; you just need a few solid ones that hold up everything else.

If you're wondering what my rules are, I honestly can't tell you. I've never written them down, but I *know* them. They guide me constantly. For example, one of mine is: *Invest in good relationships.* I can tell you that one rule does a lot of heavy lifting. It naturally filters out big, loud group events where deep connection isn't possible. It guides how I spend my time socially. It reminds me to be intentional with the people I let into my life and how I show up for them.

One rule, many outcomes.

We want to create a few guiding "rules" to help us deal with the chaos of life without becoming overwhelmed. But here's the thing: no matter how many rules we make or how carefully we plan, life will *always* be messy. There's no escaping uncertainty, but we can give ourselves a better chance of navigating it by simplifying our approach.

By embracing the unpredictability of life, we gain a greater sense of freedom. We can navigate the mess without getting caught up in the details or trying to control every outcome. You can't rulebook your way out of uncertainty. There will be chaos. Accept it.

The Art of Asking Questions

Letting go of control is not about abandoning responsibility; it's about trusting the current of life to take you where you're meant to go.

So, now that you're feeling uncomfortable, let's dive deep:

1. **What is your current approach to life? Are you comfortable flowing with the river or do you swim against the current?**
   What would it look like and feel like if you stopped trying to direct the river?

2. **How do you typically approach new relationships?**
   Are you more guarded or open to letting others show their true selves over time? What types of relationships do you currently prioritize in your life, and why?

3. **Have you ever experienced a shift in your social life, where you moved away from large gatherings to more intimate, meaningful ones?**
   What prompted that change, and how does it make you feel?

4. **Think about a time when you were surprised by someone's actions – either in a positive or negative way.**
   What does that say about your expectations of others and the role surprise plays in relationships?

5. **What are some broad principles or values that guide your decisions in life?**
   Are they flexible enough to apply in a variety of situations, or do you have specific rules that you try to follow?

There's no single formula for doing life right – but there is wisdom in simplifying your path, building sturdy internal guidelines, and staying open to what each moment might teach you.

Let the river take you. Let the rope reveal what it will. And when the time feels right, dive deep.

Chapter Seven
Let Go, or Stay Broke

When my son was young, I was running myself ragged just to keep it all together, but it wasn't serving anyone, least of all me. My "epiphany" came about six years into my business. I realized that if I were addicted to working, how could I honestly create experiences of leisure for other people?

You can't sell what you don't know. And I didn't know anything about taking time off. I was working myself into a position where I couldn't help my clients, because I didn't even understand downtime. I was my own worst enemy. So that's where the real work began: Learning not how to do more, but how to *be more* by getting off the wheel and doing less.

Most people don't know how to bridge the gap between being trapped in the hamster wheel and stepping into a life of presence, joy, and fulfillment. There's a real fear in stopping the wheel because it feels as if you do, everything will fall apart. You have bills to pay, mouths to feed, jobs to keep, and it's terrifying to imagine what happens if you let go. The entrepreneurial journey makes this even more real – how many months are there when you don't know how you're going to make payroll or pay the mortgage? It feels like everything depends on staying in motion.

But eventually you realize that all of it – money, possessions, even status – is just *stuff.*

When I was younger, I had cars repossessed, lost houses in short sales during the 2008 crash; I've gone from having the boat, the two cars, the big houses, and all the trappings to having absolutely nothing. And honestly, I wasn't any less happy being broke than I was being wealthy. What mattered was whether I knew who I was, whether I was comfortable in my own skin, and whether how I showed up for others was true and real. Everything else could come and go, and it often did.

There's no amount of planning or working that can guarantee your security because life is full of things outside of your control – death, illness, divorce. No one is exempt. The hamster wheel convinces you that you can outwork these realities, that you can plan your way to safety, but you can't. All that action ends up sacrificing the present moment for a future that may never come.

However, if you shift your focus to the relationships and the life you have right now, you start realizing that maybe, just maybe, the future will take care of itself. And even if it doesn't, you'll have lived a life that was full and real. There's tremendous freedom in realizing how much you can just let go.

I'm not saying to abandon your responsibilities, you still need to pay your bills and keep your basics covered, but if you don't add another thousand or ten thousand or even a hundred thousand dollars to your savings this month, you're probably still going to be okay. If you're still breathing, eating, and have air conditioning, especially if you live in Florida, like myself, maybe it's time to start investing a little more into your relationships and your experience of living. Remember, there's no U-Haul behind a hearse. You can't take any of it with you, so what matters is the life you live now.

I keep seeing people not living the lives they could be living because they're distracted, because they're too busy, because they're afraid. And yes, it's hard to be present sometimes for your spouse or your kid, especially when you're exhausted or burned out. But you have to push through that because the alternative is missing it all.

We cannot fully control our futures. Sure, we can influence them, but at the heart of it, we need to trust that when something inevitable happens, we'll be able to make the right decisions in that moment. Nothing is guaranteed. Not for Warren Buffett, not for Ray Dalio, not for anyone. All the money in the world can't stop death. Charlie Munger just died not too long ago. He had an incredible fortune but, by all accounts, what made him remarkable was his true sense of who he was and what mattered to him.

Elon Musk, by contrast, has unimaginable resources but comes across as someone who doesn't fully know himself, and even people close to him say he's changed beyond recognition. Money, success, none of it substitutes for having a solid sense of self.

Yet so many people stay trapped in fear: Fear of the what-ifs, fear of change, fear of stepping off the hamster wheel. Because when we step off that hamster wheel, suddenly we have to take off the mask we're wearing.

So many of us think that to "live the dream," we have to have every box checked: the salary, the house, the status … But in chasing that dream, we end up putting on a mask of success, hiding who we really are underneath what's expected of us, and when that happens, we suffer.

When we let go of those expectations and stop worrying about checking those boxes, we get a glimpse into what it's like to be free, to be alive. We become fully present, fully ourselves, and we suddenly realize we can't fit back in the box. That's the moment when everything changes.

Sometimes, the dream isn't what it seems. What we think will bring us happiness – career success, money, status – can turn out to be an empty pursuit if it's not aligned with who we truly are. Freedom comes when we stop pretending and allow ourselves to walk away from what no longer serves us.

Comfortable
with Uncomfortable

"Growth is uncomfortable
because you've never been here before.
You've never been this version of you.
So give yourself a little grace
and breathe through it."

– Kristin Lohr

It's almost oxymoronic: So many people have a fear of missing out, but they also have a fear of being uncomfortable. But the thing is, to make the most of an opportunity, to not miss out, you need to be willing to make yourself uncomfortable.

This fear runs deep in so many people, and it boils down to a lack of confidence. We don't want to commit to the unknown because what if it doesn't work out? What if things won't be okay? What if it's not how we imagined it? We stop ourselves before we've even dipped a toe in because we're worried about the outcome, and that fear makes us doubt ourselves to the point that we desperately scrape for excuses as to why we shouldn't or can't do the thing.

However, if you can truly believe that everything will work out in the end, it's so much easier to lean into uncomfortable situations, knowing that you'll be able to handle whatever comes your way.

For me, my confidence comes from knowing that I can deal with any challenge, no matter what it is. I don't walk into a situation with a pre-planned solution. I trust myself enough to know that I'll figure it out. And because of that trust, I'm not afraid to step into the unknown.

For example, it might sound strange, but if someone were to get confrontational, I won't freeze. I've learned that sometimes, the best way to reset a tense situation is with something completely unexpected. It's like when you're dealing with someone who's clearly agitated, you can say something totally random, like, "Do you know why bananas are like socks?" It's bizarre, right? But the point is that it messes with their brain. They're no longer thinking about their anger or what they wanted. Now, they're thinking, "What the hell is this person talking about?" That's enough of a distraction to reset the energy and defuse the situation.

What's amazing is that I'm not thinking of this in advance. I don't have a plan for what bizarre thing I'll say, but I know I can do it. And that confidence comes from the experiences I've had – the times when I've been in uncomfortable or strange situations and had to figure it out on the fly.

Those situations have taught me skills that I draw on whenever I'm faced with uncertainty. The only way to build that confidence is by putting yourself in situations where you don't know what's going to happen. Because if you never do that, you're always going to be scared of it.

And that's a cycle you'll never break. If you let fear control your reactions, then that fear will always own you. You won't be the one in control of the situation; the situation will be in control of you.

What does "sexy" even mean?

Random, right? But trust me, I have a point.

Think about it. What does "sexy" mean to you? There are so many opinions about what makes someone attractive: a certain body type, certain features, even the car they drive. People say it's all about the butt, the legs, the boobs, and so on. But I think at the core, real sex appeal comes from confidence.

I've seen people who are bigger in size but exude confidence, and honestly, it's magnetic. And on the flip side, I've also seen supermodels with "perfect" bodies, by society's standards, with no confidence. They're withdrawn, unsure of themselves, and it's impossible to connect with them. There's no energy, no spark.

Confidence is about operating in life, through time and space, in places where you're unsure, or where the outcome is uncertain. You don't just get it instantly, though. Confidence is earned, and it comes from stepping into uncomfortable situations, or even especially when you don't know exactly what will happen.

When I was 18, I spent six months as an exchange student in Barcelona. My parents gave me some money to buy a new pair of rollerblades. It was the 90s; rollerblading was the thing to do. I had 150 euros in my pocket, which I was dying to spend on these new blades. One day, I was walking around near the Las Ramblas area when I came across a guy doing the classic three-card monte trick with shells and a ball. This old lady was trying to follow the game, but she kept picking the wrong shell, even though the guy was so bad at it that you could literally see where the ball was. I thought, *I've got this. I can spot the trick.*

But no, I ended up falling for it. One hundred and fifty euros later, I walked away with the realization that I had been completely tricked. I went into that situation confident that I would never be fooled. But I came out of it feeling like an idiot. It was an uncomfortable lesson, but one I'll never forget.

Some people would look at that situation and think, "See? That's why I would never do anything like that." But here's the thing: There's always something valuable in discomfort.

It's like when someone shows you a magic trick. At first, you're amazed. Then they reveal how it's done, and the mystery is gone. The next time you see the trick, it's not impressive anymore. You know the trick. The same goes for life. If you don't go out and experience the unexpected, you'll never know the magic of truly understanding what's possible.

By putting yourself in uncomfortable situations. You stop living in the bubble of the "filtered" experience. You start seeing things for what they really are, and in doing so, you start living life fully, confidently, and without hesitation.

Say F*ck It

How many people do we know who have different versions of themselves? How many versions do you have of yourself? We've got a public version, a family version, a work version ... We're constantly trying to pretend like we're water, just fitting into whatever vase happens to be there.

When I graduated from college, I had my list of markers for success, right? Buy a house, make $100,000-plus a year, tick off all these things that I thought meant I had made it. By the time I was 26, I had hit every single one of those markers, and honestly, it felt kind of empty. Sure, I had the house and the money and all the stuff, but I wasn't any happier than when I didn't have them.

I went through about twelve years of bouncing around, just moving from one thing I was good at to the next without ever really feeling happy with any of it. At 34 years old, I finally had enough.

I was working as a mortgage broker, helping people refinance their high interest rates, sitting in a cubicle, making 100 calls a day, just searching for that one person willing to talk to me and get something done. I did help some people, and that felt good, but after a while, I realized I was on the same hamster wheel as I was before.

It was exactly the same as when I was a finance manager at a car dealership, except I didn't make as much money, and it wasn't as predictable. The sales cycle was longer, and I couldn't influence things the way I used to. Back then, I would call a bank and say, "Hey, I know this client's credit is terrible, but I want you to approve this loan anyway. I'll bring you five or ten other great deals to make up for it." And they'd be like, "Sure."

Mortgage broking was a whole different ball game. So, you'd be working on a loan for 45 days, only to find out two or three days before closing that the deal is off. And you'd be sitting there thinking, *What the hell?* After 45 days of work, it's just … gone. And now the client's pissed. It's frustrating. Not to mention, it just didn't feel right. It wasn't the work I was looking for. There was money in it. But deep down, I knew it wasn't me. So, I finally said, "F*ck it."

I realized I had made money, lost money, done impressive things, failed at things, and none of it truly mattered. For the first time in my life, I sat down and asked myself, "What do I actually want to do?"

I had no clue.

Unsurprisingly, it's really difficult to answer questions you've never asked yourself before.

So, my first "really bad" idea was that I was going to become a ski instructor in the French Alps. I was three weeks away from selling all my stuff, moving there with no job lined up, intent to figure it out as I went. My mom was, of course, not thrilled by this plan. But I had this sense of confidence and faith in myself. I trusted that I would find a way to make it work, even if it wasn't pretty. Tenacity was something I had in spades.

However, around that time, my mom happened to see this article in *France* magazine about a guy who had owned a real estate agency in Colorado for twenty years, sold everything, and moved to France to start a ski school. It was eerily similar to what I was about to do, so I tracked the guy down and wrote him a ridiculously long email. In short, I basically said, "I'm where you must have been. I'm ready to blow up the game and do something real."

The next day, this total stranger spent four hours on the phone with me, hearing my story and telling me his.

He said, "I get it. But you don't get it." He explained that you can't just decide to become a ski instructor in France – it's a five-year schooling process, and I'd be almost 40 by the time I was certified and just starting a career. But then he said, "You sound smart. Why don't you just get people to come here and ski instead? You could be a tour operator."

I'd traveled around the world eight times, lived in multiple countries, and still had no idea what a tour operator even was. Most people don't. They think of travel agents, but those are just the middlemen. Tour operators are the ones who actually design the experiences, every touch, taste, activity, everything you feel. It's a higher level of responsibility, a different kind of business altogether.

So instead of three weeks, I spent four weeks studying the industry obsessively. I researched the market, the players, what it would take … And after all that, I realized that I didn't just want to sell ski vacations. I wanted to be a luxury tour operator, someone who created transformative experiences. I realized I was good at encouraging people to step out of their comfort zones and do things they'd later be grateful for, so I leaned into that. At the time, I was on unemployment, making $1,100 a month; it wasn't exactly glamorous. I decided to move back in with my parents at 34 years old, and for the next year, I went all in. This wasn't a "try" thing – this was my Plan A, B, and C. No fallback plan.

Somewhere in the beginning of that process, an acquaintance from high school reached out to me out of the blue and said, "Hey, my wife and I are celebrating our 10-year anniversary. Can you plan something for us?" Without hesitation, I said yes, even though I still had no real idea how to price anything or what I was doing. It ended up being an $18,000 custom tour, and I pretty much spent every dollar making sure they had an unforgettable experience.

I didn't profit at all on that first job, but almost fourteen years later, they're still my clients.

That was the beginning. It wasn't easy, it wasn't clean, and there were plenty of mistakes. But that's part of it. As long as you're okay with making mistakes and actually learning from them, you'll be fine. That's how you build a life that means something, because sometimes you just have to turn around and say, "F*ck it."

The first step to living a fuller life is to stop playing the role that others expect. Instead, start showing up as your truest self in every situation. *You don't have to be everything to everyone. You just need to be enough for yourself.* It may feel uncomfortable at first, but it's only through embracing authenticity that you'll discover a deeper sense of satisfaction and happiness. And you don't have to have all the answers now – I know I sure as hell didn't. Just trust yourself to pivot when you need to, because it's not about having a concrete plan at every moment. It's about trusting that you have the ability to figure it out as you go.

The Art of Asking Questions

Life challenges you to ask the hard questions, and more often than not, you won't like the answers you find to those questions. But if you avoid asking them and stay where you are, you're going to go broke.

Sometimes you have to let go of what you know in order to move forward.

But before you move forward with this book, ask yourself:

1. **When have you ever found yourself overworking in an attempt to "have it all"?**
   How did it affect your relationships and overall happiness? What aspects of your life feel most disconnected from who you truly are?

2. **What fears did you have about taking time off or stepping back from the constant busyness, and how did those fears influence your decisions?**
   How can you challenge those fears moving forward?

3. **What areas in your life could you push yourself to get uncomfortable in order to build confidence?**
   How do you balance preparing for the future with accepting the uncertainty and unpredictability of life?

4. **Have you ever had an "epiphany moment" that shifted your perspective on life or success?**
   How did it change the course of your life, and are there any lingering questions you still need to explore?

5. **What does "saying F*ck it" mean to you in your current life?**
   Consider what it would look like for you to stop following the rules you've set for yourself or those imposed by others. What would you need to let go of to fully embrace your true self?

Growth happens in the messiness of life, and the courage to embrace that messiness is where true freedom lies. Trust that the process, however uncomfortable, will lead you closer to the life you were meant to live.

PART III
The System of Soul
Living Fully, While You Can

For a long time, I believed the goal was to build a big life – more success, more work, more movement. I thought if I just pushed harder, achieved more, stayed busy enough, I'd end up somewhere that felt meaningful. But life has a way of holding up a mirror. Getting married made me realize how easy it is to mistake commitment for connection. Having a son changed the way I viewed time. And being diagnosed with Parkinson's? That turned every assumption on its head. Suddenly, every moment had weight. Every decision about how I spent my time felt sharper, more urgent, more real.

So take this as your invitation to pause long enough to ask whether the life you're building is actually one you want to live. Because the truth is, most of us don't need more hustle; we need more presence. More connection. More meaning. And most importantly, more honesty about where our energy is going and whether it's bringing us any closer to who we really are.

But you don't need a crisis to start asking these questions. You can choose to be intentional with your time before life forces you to be. You can learn to sit in stillness without panic.

You can rediscover what makes you curious, what brings you joy, and what kind of life actually feels worth living.

You may not be able to control the clock, but you can choose how you show up inside of it. So take a breath. Put the noise on mute. And let's talk about what it really means to live, *fully, freely, and on purpose,* while you still can.

Chapter Eight
The Experience
is the Product

"The best things in life aren't things."

– Art Buchwald

Luxury travel hasn't really changed in over 60 years. Originally, you'd thumb through glossy brochures in a travel agent's office, decide on a destination, and then start a months-long back-and-forth. Today, the brochures live online, but the process is virtually the same: You fill out a web form, wait for someone to call you (if they ever do), schedule a one-to-two-hour phone interview, and then, after three to five business days, receive a single proposal. Change the dates, hotels, guides, or anything else, and you wait another three to five days. This process rinses and repeats until you have a plan, usually taking three weeks from start to finish.

Here's the thing: If someone were beginning to plan five to six months before their tour, a three-week process would be no big deal. But the truth is that most people know how stressful it is to plan a vacation, and so they don't even begin planning until two to three months before they want to go. The stress of that three-week transaction leads most people to do what people do best: They hit the easy button and choose a bad plan over no plan at all.

For example, it means they will choose a cruise, an all-inclusive resort, or they will go somewhere they have been before.

All of these options are easier, but they don't take advantage of the opportunities that could enhance their experience and expand their life.

So, in a world where we can get a package delivered in two days or even two hours, who wants to wait three weeks to get information about their vacation?

We saw that and thought there had to be a better way. Our answer was to build a truly "no-waiting" experience: Pick your destination from over twenty countries on our site, choose from over 75 curated tours, and click "Get My Itinerary." No phone call required. You receive a complete, fully-priced proposal in about 10 minutes that's valid for travel on any date this year or next – no blackout periods, no hidden fees, no endless back-and-forth. You simply tell us when you want to go after you accept the proposal, during your onboarding meeting. In less than an afternoon, you can go from "I'd like to vacation" to "I'm on my way," with zero stress.

Every journey starts the moment you walk out your front door. We include a private car anytime you have your luggage with you, including when you leave your house, and with English-speaking drivers we ensure that you're able to communicate if for any reason you'd like to stop. You stay in at least a four-star property (with easy upgrades into our prestige five-star "platinum" category), plus daily breakfast and an automatic one-category room upgrade so you're never squeezed into the tiniest room. We kick off your trip with a welcome dinner, because the first meal in a new country should never be an afterthought, and cap it with a farewell dinner to send you off without last-night packing panic.

Each city includes one privately guided tour with skip-the-line access, tailored to what you want to see. In destinations where visitors usually have very specific goals, like the Vatican in Rome or the gorilla treks in Rwanda, we pack multiple highlights into a single day. Between these essentials, you're free to explore at your own pace or choose from our "Savor" (our foodie package), "Explore" (our culture category), "Pampered" (if you want utmost luxury), and "Excite" (if you want something more adrenaline-filled) add-ons. For example, with our packages, you can experience anything from winery tastings and Michelin-starred meals, spa treatments and personal shoppers, hot-air balloons and Ferrari drives, historic walking tours, all with your own private and professional paparazzi to capture every incredible moment.

You'll see the exact price on screen, add any extras you like, submit your details, and voilà: your luxury, bespoke itinerary is ready to go.

And after, the flights and travel insurance are organized with our assistance. At every stage, we make sure all the little touches are taken care of so that you don't have to stress. Because that's the secret sauce: eliminating the waiting, simplifying the choices, handling every high-stress pinch point from doorstep to farewell. You get more than a trip; you get the freedom to be present for every moment, without the usual scramble. And no brochure or "advanced AI" algorithm can replicate that.

Reconnecting with Past Lives

I have the privilege of helping people to live – to really experience life to the fullest. Many of my clients save up for years to employ me to make it happen for them. They understand that these experiences are rare and worth the "sacrifice." And then there are those with ample means, who say they would have paid triple for what we just did. But regardless of financial standing, the effect is always profound. From the experiences we provide, people come back fulfilled, happy, and perhaps more interested in things they didn't even know existed before.

Traveling exposes you to different cultures, to how other people solve their common problems, and it often leaves you with a calmer, more patient mindset. This ripple effect touches everyone around you in the days, weeks, and even months that follow.

For example, one of our clients was heading to Belgium with their family, and I told them, "I want you to take a day from your trip and go to the World War I battlefields." They were hesitant, unsure. "Why do we want to do that?" But I knew they *needed* to.

World War I fascinates me far more than World War II. WWII is often at the forefront of our minds, but WWI was the moment when everything changed – the intersection of old traditions with new technologies.

It was the first war where airplanes, machine guns, and gas warfare were introduced. It was also the last war where soldiers on horseback charged into the fray only to be slaughtered by gunfire. It's an incredibly intense, tragic moment in history, and yet, it was foundational to the inevitable events of World War II.

For 6,000 years, every single bit of knowledge, every story of wars and victories and defeats and everything else in between, was passed down through generations. It was all oral history until World War I. The horrors of that war were so vast, the losses so catastrophic, that those who survived didn't speak about it. And because of that silence, their children entered WWII without truly understanding what their parents had gone through. The trauma was so intense, it couldn't be shared, and that pattern continued, creating what's now called the "Silent Generation."

For the first time in human history, we lost the direct transmission of lived experience. What we now know about these wars comes from historians, textbooks, and facts pulled from the internet. The personal stories, the ones that shape how we understand history, have largely disappeared. This loss of oral history is something I find deeply troubling. We don't have the lived context from those who were actually there, and it has left us disconnected from the very real experiences of our ancestors.

Our generation, and those coming after us, have seen an enormous shift in the transfer of information. We are living in the Digital Age after all, and so if we want something, we go online – or if you want to be really up-to-date, we go to AI. AI has, for many people, become their sole source of information, more so than search engines. Why are dolphins mammals? What is the capital of South Africa? When was the Tower of London built? How do I bake a gluten-free, nut-free chocolate cake? If we have a query, we ask a computer instead of a real person. So, if we want to know about World War I or II, why not turn to digital sources, like ChatGPT, rather than speaking to someone who lived through it?

But here's the thing: How much richer would our understanding be if we could hear those stories from the people who were there?

That's why I consider these trips not just as vacations, but as opportunities to reconnect with a history we're losing. Every single person I've sent to one of these kinds of locations on their custom experience, despite their initial reluctance, has come back with a profound sense of appreciation and insight. When you stand before an ossuary in Verdun, where the bones of unidentified soldiers are collected, you realize the weight of what these people died for: freedom, the fight against fascism, and the preservation of their way of life. You can't walk away from that without being deeply moved.

But the real tragedy is that we often seem to be forgetting the lessons these sacrifices taught us. Many people don't understand civics, don't recognize the history that shaped their current freedoms. And that's where the ripple effect of experiencing history comes into play. These moments force you to consider the broader implications, to reflect on the values that keep society stable, and to pass those lessons on to the next generation.

It's why I feel so strongly about the importance of sharing these experiences. Remember, we offered the genealogy package to reconnect people with their histories, to let them explore their roots as far back as possible and see the whole story. So, whether it's traveling to Europe, learning about history firsthand, or simply engaging with the world in new ways, these moments matter. Because if we don't understand these things, we're doomed to repeat them.

Expanding Your Mindset

For people who are used to being in charge of everything – making all the decisions, booking their own vacations, and being in control at work – letting go of the reins can be one of the hardest things they ever do. And even if you only feel like you need to be in control of one or two things, it's still not easy to give that over to someone else.

For example, in my business, people come to me to book their out-of-this-world experience, but to do that, they have to give over control. We organize everything for them, right down to the finest detail so that all they have to do is show up and relax. Sometimes when people give it a try, come back saying it was the best experience they've had, and then … I don't hear from them again. Sometimes it's just hard for people to escape their own inertia. But I do stay in contact with them, and there are people who've come around in the long run.

One client, a labor relations manager for Publix, had an incredible trip with his wife. Seven years later, he wrote me a glowing review, saying how much they still remember the experience and how often they talk about it.

However, the reality is that a lot of people try to find excuses not to go on vacation, especially the kind I offer, because they don't want to give up control.

They create this cycle for themselves, depriving themselves of opportunity, but as soon as they take the chance, let go of the reins, and experience the trip, they see the value. Even though it was more than they sometimes expect to spend, they realize this was exactly what they wanted.

People often fixate on saving money as if it's the only lens through which to view a trip – but let's examine that mindset for a moment: What's the cheapest vacation you can have? Seriously, think about it. You could go all-inclusive, but that's still money. How about a cheap motel for a night? Nope, still money, right? What about if you just stayed home, how much would you be spending to do that?

Exactly.

If your goal is to save money, don't go on vacation at all.

But if you decide to go, then everything shifts to *value*. It's no longer about how much something costs; it's about what kind of experience you're going to have. You could stay in a cheap motel to save money, but your experience will suffer. And the whole point of a vacation is the *experience*. It's the actual antithesis of every other financial transaction you're going to make. It becomes an investment in life, not just of money.

For example, if you need a blue shirt, you can look at one priced at $100 and one priced at $20. You can buy the cheaper option because, at the end of the day, it's still a blue shirt. It might not be as well made as the $100 one, or last as long, but if all you need is a blue shirt, why not go for the cheap option?

You can't do that with a vacation. You have to change your mindset from "How can I save money?" to "What kind of experience am I going to have?"

Last year, I arranged a birthday dinner cruise on the Thames in London for a client. What they didn't know was that I had arranged for the band on board to play his favorite song – just for him. It was going to be a special, memorable moment. But the clients didn't pick up their phone when I called multiple times to let them know the pick-up time was adjusted due to traffic. I probably called six or seven times, my partners in England also tried to get a hold of them, and by the time I did get a hold of them – by calling their driver and getting him to hand the phone to them – it was too late. They were going to miss the whole experience, but there was nothing I could do.

In the end, they spent an extra $300 on dinner because they missed the cruise and then wanted me to refund them for the missed experience. But why were they not picking up the phone? They didn't want to risk phone charges. They saved $15, but it cost them far more in the long run.

I've had similar situations with clients wanting to save on taxi fares, so they walked and missed out on important experiences. People can often be their own worst enemies when it comes to fully embracing the value of the experience they're paying for.

It really does all come down to what you value more: experience or money. If you value money above everything else, you're likely to measure everything from a financial perspective, which is how most people are conditioned to think. But when you choose experiences over money, there's a bit of a cycle that can result in you falling back into the money-centered mindset. You need money to have those experiences, but the real question is, how do you balance the two?

We care so much about our clients having the best experience they can, we created a course to teach them how to better plan for a tour of their own that they can build. We give them the resources to have a great trip, even when we can't plan it within the budget they have.

What we do isn't for everyone. At some point, I'd love to build a separate brand that caters to a wider audience by making our services accessible to a lot more people while still delivering a great experience. Because the key to helping people give themselves permission to fully immerse themselves in and enjoy an experience is to solve all the little problems that typically create friction.

For example, how long does it take to get the information? Just 10 minutes. If you want to change your travel dates, no problem. With most companies, you'd have to go back and forth, and they might tell you the new dates will cost more. Not with us. We've removed that friction, because the goal is to get the right information to you quickly.

We've also tackled the common travel questions that often cause stress: Do you need adapters? What should you pack? What should you wear? With us, these concerns are taken care of. When people travel to another country and feel uneasy, what makes them feel secure is knowing that everything has been accounted for. All they need to do is show up at the lobby and meet their guide. There's nothing scary about that.

It's all about giving them security and comfortability so that they release control and trust that everything has been handled.

When people feel confident that every little detail is handled – from what to pack to where to go – it creates the kind of trust that lets them fully embrace the experience. And that trust shouldn't start on the first day of the trip; it should start the moment someone starts planning. But here's the problem: For most people, even getting a proposal from a travel agency is a hassle. It's time-consuming, expensive, and often leaves people feeling like they're just part of a sales pipeline, not someone whose needs are actually being heard.

With other agencies, lot of time, energy, and money go into creating these proposals. It costs hundreds of dollars per proposal to produce, so if you're the one who books a tour, you're the one paying for the nine other people who got a proposal but didn't book. At other agencies, this is all built into the pricing, but as the customer, you don't know that. You're not getting a better experience – it's just money being shifted around to facilitate the process. It doesn't improve your actual experience.

We do things differently.

We don't have the same restrictions and dogma that other companies have. Our system is automated, which means the cost to provide you with a proposal is less than $1. Because of this, we don't limit you to one proposal. If you want to compare Greece, Italy, Peru, and Tahiti, no problem. Check them all out. With us, you're not going to pay for someone else's indecision.

I had a client a couple of months ago who pulled four different proposals. It's rare, but it happened. He had two proposals for Italy, one for Paris, and one for the UK. When he called me, he said, "I want you to explain one of these." I asked, "Which one?" He replied, "Any of them." So, I explained the options. At the end of the conversation, he said, "Stop. I want you to take all four tours and combine them into one 34-day tour for my goddaughters."

What started as a short trip with a single destination quickly turned into a multi-destination tour because he wanted his goddaughters to have the best experience.

This process would have taken him hours of research and multiple back-and-forth conversations, potentially over several days, just to get a proposal. With me, he was done in a few days. We took three or four days to custom-create the trip, making sure everything was priced and logistically aligned. And just like that, he was ready to go.

The key difference here is that I focus on providing maximum value. We charge a fair price, but we offer a much higher level of service than most other companies. We're able to give clients an extraordinary experience without them needing to spend a fortune. It's all about trust. Clients trust us to filter out the noise and tell them exactly what they need to know.

And everyone has a budget, including billionaires; it just depends on whether their budget is financial or mental. Some people are fine spending a significant amount on one thing but would never consider spending the same on something else. For example, some might balk at spending $20,000 on a Birkin bag but have no problem spending that amount on a car or on a vacation. It's all a mental game, and what you have to be able to do is open yourself to opportunity without thinking about that budget in the back of your mind – because when you do, you open yourself up to what's truly possible.

The Art of Asking Questions

Growth doesn't happen when everything goes according to plan. It happens in the in-between spaces. In the delays, the disruptions, the breakdowns. It happens when you're stuck in traffic on the way to what was supposed to be a perfect weekend. Or when the job you thought you wanted turns out to be a box with no air. Or when you realize the version of success you've been chasing doesn't actually feel that good.

That's where questions matter. So before you jump into the next chapter, stop and ask yourself:

1. **How do you typically approach major decisions in your life?**
   Do you find yourself frustrated with long processes or delays, and how do you cope with them?

2. **How do you personally feel about letting go of control when it comes to vacations or major experiences?**
   What can you learn from being less in control?

3. **How often do you settle for convenience in your life, whether in your personal, work, or travel experiences?**
   What do you think is lost when you choose ease over depth?

4. **How do you handle situations where things don't go as planned?**

   Do you focus on minimizing losses, or do you look for the value in unexpected outcomes?

5. **When making big decisions, how often do you consider the long-term impact on your life and happiness versus short-term gains or material rewards?**

   How do you currently, and how could you better balance the two?

Don't wait for the perfect moment to do what you want to do. Don't tell yourself you'll do X once the kids are older, once work slows down, once you've saved a little more. Life doesn't wait. Neither should you.

Chapter Nine
Get Tactical

If you never leave your business, you never really know whether it can survive without you. This is something that most business owners and entrepreneurs don't learn until it's too late.

That's where the idea of tactical vacationing comes in. Step away from your business, intentionally, not reactively, with the specific goal of seeing what breaks in your absence. You don't just disappear; you go on vacation with your eyes open. Then, when you return, you fix what failed. You build better systems, tighter processes. Then you do it again – another vacation, a little longer this time.

Repeat this often enough, and one day, you'll realize you can be gone for a month, maybe even longer, and everything still runs just fine.

That's the mark of a successful business. Not how much it needs you, but how little. And as strange as it sounds, it's that very distance that allows you to start seeing your work in a new way. When you're not knee-deep in the day-to-day grind, you finally have the space to think strategically. You stop reacting and start designing. You move from being the operator to becoming the architect.

People who do tactical vacationing well don't just regain their time, they regain perspective.

Sometimes, stepping away teaches you that certain tasks don't need doing at all. Maybe you delegate something to a part-time virtual assistant – $500 a month to buy back 30 or 40 hours of your time. Or maybe you eliminate that task altogether because, frankly, it wasn't that important to begin with. If your business or your life can't absorb a small monthly investment to offload the busywork, it's often not just a cost issue; it's a priority issue.

I've seen the opposite play out, too.

My mom has run a commercial real estate business for over 25 years. She's built deep client relationships and had a successful run, but now that she's thinking about retirement, she's discovered something hard: Her business is unsellable. There are no systems, no processes – just her. She *is* the business.

And while that may have worked fine for her in the short term, it's a cautionary tale. If you can't duplicate yourself, if you can't ever leave without the entire thing collapsing, then everything you've built may die with you.

100% of business owners will exit their business. The only question is *how*. Will you leave because you planned for it, created something sustainable, and handed it off with intention?

Or will your exit be an accident, through burnout, crisis, or death, leaving nothing behind but fragments?

Tactical vacationing isn't about taking more time off just to lounge around. It's about designing a business, and a life, that functions without you as its single point of failure. And it's about reclaiming time to invest in what truly matters.

Because at the end of it all, your real legacy won't be the business itself. It'll be the people you shared your life with. The relationships you built. The memories you made. Not the meetings you scheduled or the emails you sent, but the experiences you lived, and the space you created for others to grow.

That's what lasts.

No End to Work?
It's Your Choice

At first, stepping away from work feels bleak. If your identity has been wrapped up entirely in being productive, then the moment you stop, even for a weekend, it can feel like you're completely unbalanced. Like a toddler trying to walk for the first time, you'll stumble. You'll suck at it. You won't know what to do with your time, and that's when the trap appears.

The trap is this: You try taking time off, but it feels empty or aimless. You don't instantly find some exciting, soul-enriching hobby. And so you conclude, "Well, I guess I don't really have anything else I like," and just like that, you dive right back into work. It's like a black hole that pulls you in – familiar, consuming, and endlessly deep.

To break free, you have to give it time. You have to retrain your brain to rediscover curiosity, to explore again. It might be something simple, like reading more, going for a walk, or investing in your health. It could mean building new relationships, or, if you're still wired for structure, maybe you join a country club – not for status, but for connection. Maybe you like golf. Maybe you don't. Maybe you just want to sit and have a meal with someone who isn't part of your daily grind.

The point is to expose yourself to other ways of living. To explore what life could look like when it isn't jammed to the brim with tasks and deadlines.

Because here's what no one tells you: There is no end to work. No matter how much you do, there's always more waiting. You can work all day and still go to bed with a to-do list whispering in your ear.

I learned that the hard way, especially when my son was born. I started becoming really selective about what work I actually did. I used to believe everything on my list was critical. But when time got tight, I had to start making hard choices – and nothing fell apart. In fact, most of the things I let go of just ... disappeared. No disaster. No meltdown. They just quietly stopped being done, and it didn't matter.

That was a massive shift for me. So much of the work we think is "essential" is actually optional. It only feels important because we've trained ourselves to never stop moving.

Sure, there are things with real deadlines – deliverables that affect clients or people depending on you – but beyond that? The rest is just endless filler. An infinite bucket of "I could do this" tasks: Write another newsletter, reach out to this contact, brainstorm that campaign. The list regenerates every time you cross something off.

And that's the part we all need to learn: The work will never be done. The bucket will never be full.

So the real question becomes, *when do you stop trying to fill it?*

When do you finally give yourself permission to do something else, not because it's productive, not because it's efficient, but because it's meaningful?

That's the path I'm still walking. And I know this much: You have to take that first, clumsy step out of the black hole. You have to learn, slowly, how to be someone *outside* of work. And eventually, if you let yourself, you'll discover there's a whole life waiting for you on the other side.

Have Faith in Yourself

"Sometimes the hardest part

isn't letting go

but learning to start over."

– Nicole Sobon

A lot of people stay stuck in survival mode because they're afraid. Afraid that something's going to knock them off track. Afraid they'll lose their business. Afraid they'll end up with no money. So they stay in control. They plan. They overwork. They tell themselves they're just being responsible.

But what they're really trying to do is future-proof their life. And here's the uncomfortable truth: You can't.

There is *no* future-proofing. That's an illusion. A comforting one, sure, but still an illusion. Control is something we think we have, but when it comes to the future? We're guessing. We're hoping. We're pretending we know what's coming next. But the future doesn't care about your plan.

Just look around. Right now, there are a million truck drivers out there. My dad was one of them for over 20 years. When I told him that self-driving trucks were coming, he didn't believe me. He said, "That's never going to happen."

But it *is* happening. It's already underway in places like Texas. It's real. And it's going to change everything.

Same goes for lawyers. Same goes for accountants. There are people in law school right now chasing a career that AI is already beginning to encroach on. No, it's not replacing every task, but it's changing the game. I can get a decent contract from ChatGPT. It's not perfect, but it's usable.

And this isn't doomsaying. This is about facing reality. Tomorrow doesn't exist. Yesterday doesn't exist. The only thing that's real is *right now*.

The problem is that our brains want to feel safe. That's what drives this obsession with control. But often, it's just a performance. TSA makes us take our shoes off at the airport. Does that really make us safer? Not really. But it *feels* like it does. It's safety theater. And that's what a lot of our future-proofing is: an illusion of protection that doesn't actually protect.

So what should you do instead?

Well, when you're stuck in survival mode, you can't always see it for what it is: This endless loop of control, overwork, and fear. Maybe it's rooted in something deep: a fear of poverty, a history of scarcity, or a belief that if they stop, everything will fall apart. Maybe it's simple inertia or habit. For anyone in that place, the first step isn't about action.

It's about realization. You have to start by admitting that whatever you're doing right now isn't working. Where you are right now – mentally, emotionally, financially, relationally – isn't where you want to be. That awareness is the foundation of any real change. If you can honestly say, "I'm not where I want to be," then you've already taken the first step out of survival mode.

After that?

Start doing things differently.

It doesn't matter *what* you do differently at first – just that you do something new. If you've been zigging, start zagging. Take a different route. Try something unexpected. Don't overthink it, and don't wait for the perfect strategy. The goal is simply to disrupt the pattern that's keeping you stuck.

Think of it like cracking a safe. You won't know the right combination until you start spinning the dial. But when you hear that click, when something lands, you'll know. It'll feel right. The pieces will align, and it will be obvious.

But none of that can happen if you're still doing what you've always done, hoping for different results. That's the biggest trap. People often keep repeating the same choices, even when they know those choices aren't delivering the life they want. It feels safer, sure—but safety doesn't always lead to fulfillment.

There's no magic pill. No universal five-step plan that works for everyone. The truth is much simpler and harder: You have to choose change, and you have to keep choosing it until something clicks.

It won't feel easy. And that's okay. Just don't confuse being busy with being in control, or being exhausted with being on the right path. Control is not the goal – *freedom is*. And you can't build freedom by chaining yourself to the same habits that kept you stuck.

So start with the smallest move in a new direction. Try anything. Change the pattern. Let the lock click. And when it does, walk through that open door with faith in yourself.

You've had faith in yourself before, so trust me when I say, you can find it again.

Don't believe me?

Take a moment and think back to the hardest moments in your life – when you were broke, when you were hustling, when you weren't sure how you'd get by. But you *did*. Maybe you were waiting tables, stocking shelves, sweeping floors. You figured it out.

And you'll do it again, if you need to.

You don't need to plan for every possible outcome. You just need to remember that you've already proven to yourself that you're capable.

I have a friend who's a licensed attorney. After a long and well-paid career, she walked away from law entirely. Now? She works on helping spaceports get funding across the States. It sounds random, right? But she had faith in her skills. She trusted that she could pivot. And she did.

The truth is, you don't need to figure out the future right now, because the future hasn't happened yet.

What you *can* do now is take a step back and start asking real questions about who you are. What matters to you? What do you love? What are you curious about? If you never ask those questions, you won't be ready when change *does* happen. You'll be like a toddler learning to walk, starting from scratch.

But if you start now, start getting to know yourself, start loosening your grip on control, you'll be building something more useful than a five-year plan. You'll be building trust in *you*. And that's the only kind of future-proofing that actually works.

The Art of Asking Questions

While this chapter has a focus on the business side of things, the lessons here can be applied to any aspect of your life. Anyone can find themselves in survival mode – in fact, most people do. The idea is to release control, break your patterns, and discover what is truly meaningful in your life. Because, trust me, when you really think about it, it's not going to be work.

Take a moment to think about it, and ask yourself:

1. **What would break in your business or life if you stepped away for two weeks?**
   What would happen if it breaks, and if you already know it's broken, why hasn't it been fixed yet?

2. **Are you holding on to certain tasks because they're truly essential, or because they make you feel important?**
   Why do you think this way?

3. **When was the last time you did something just because it was meaningful?**
   I'm not talking about something that was productive or that you "needed" to get done; I'm talking about something you wanted to do, that gave you a deeper sense of fulfillment and achievement. Knowing this, has your answer changed?

4. **What pattern in your life or work needs disrupting – and what small step could you take today to shift it?**
   And imagine the possibilities that will open up when you take it.

5. **Do you trust your ability to adapt if everything changed tomorrow?**
   This is a hard question to sit with, but really think about it. No matter what your answer, be sure to ask yourself why you think that way.

Remember, you've done hard things before. You'll do them again. So instead of clinging to what's safe, start asking what's true. That's the path to building not just a business that runs without you – but a life that fulfills you.

Chapter Ten
Your Time, Reclaimed

"You know, why we're here?
To be out, this is out ... and
out is one of the single most
enjoyable experiences of life."

– Seinfeld

When I worked at the Hyundai-Buick dealership, I stepped into the role of finance manager. That in itself was unusual, because most finance managers work their way up from sales. But here I was, skipping straight to the position I wanted without going through the steps everyone else had to take. It was the second time I'd done that in my career – and honestly, since then, it's something I've pulled off more than a few times.

My mentor there was the other finance manager. He'd been in the business a long time; he was a great guy, someone who had really been through it all. He was a recovering alcoholic and drug addict, and his rock bottom came when he lost custody of his kids and his wife left him. He'd never been arrested, which is kind of rare given the spiral he described, but somehow he pulled himself out of it.

On his own. He quit drinking, quit drugs, and completely turned his life around. So much so that he ended up serving on the board of a halfway house, helping guide other people on their recovery journeys.

One of my favorite stories he ever told me came from his time in AA. He said, "You know, when you're in AA long enough, the stories get repetitive. Everyone thinks their story is so unique, but they start to sound the same."

He told me about one meeting where they had a guest speaker coming in. He was excited, thinking this person might bring something fresh, something meaningful. But the story ended up being more of the same.

So I asked, "Did you take anything away from it?"

He pointed to the ashtray on his desk. "I took that."

I was confused. "The ashtray?"

He grinned. "Yeah. When I first started AA, my mentor told me, 'You should always take something from a meeting.' So I did. I took the ashtray."

The point is every situation has *something* to offer, but not every situation has to spark an epiphany. Sometimes, the takeaway is small, or funny, or just a reminder that not everything needs to be deep. Sometimes, all you walk away with is … the ashtray.

This idea of reclaiming time and finding meaning, even in the small things, stuck with me. It's something that happens to all of us: We start gaining time, whether through better systems, delegating tasks, or automating processes – and then we give that time right back to work. We find new tasks, lean in more, and stay busy because we don't know what else to do. That newly available time starts to feel like a void, and we fill it with more of the one thing we know ... Work.

But here's the question we *should* be asking: What does it mean to reclaim your time in a way that actually builds a good life? One that's still productive. Still meaningful. But also fulfilling?

The answer starts with a catalyst – something that forces you to ask, "Am I spending my time in the right places?"

When I was in my 20s, I had no wife, no kid. I had my work life and my weekend life, and not much in between. There wasn't any reason for change. No pressure to evolve. No need to reflect.

But getting married? That changed things. Suddenly, I had to ask myself, "Am I investing in this relationship? Or did I just sign a contract and call it love?" Because those are *not* the same thing.

Then I had a child. And that changed things even more.

You start thinking about the "18 summers," after all, you only get 18 of them with your kid. Eighteen chances to really be present. That number is smaller than we think. And it matters.

Now, for me, getting diagnosed with Parkinson's became another one of those catalysts. It changes how I view my time, my body, and my future. It makes me reassess where my energy is going.

But here's the truth: You shouldn't wait for a life-altering event to reassess how you spend your time. Not everyone gets that loud wake-up call.

If you *don't* have a major catalyst, create a small one. Donate time to a cause. Take on a new hobby. Not a distraction – like zoning out in front of Call of Duty – but something that creates something inside you. Something that requires you to learn, grow, invest in yourself. It could be painting, woodworking, building model trains, designing custom LEGO sets, or planting a garden. Something creative. Something that asks something of you. That helps you get to know yourself better.

It's a bit like how Michelangelo sculpted – not from all angles at once, but front to back, carving away what wasn't necessary until the form revealed itself. That's what using your reclaimed time can look like. You try things. You peel away what doesn't fit. What's left is *you* – the real you.

Our future is changing, fast. I watched a video recently of a UK grocery fulfillment center that's completely automated. The robots do everything except deliver the groceries. And it's not just an isolated case. With the development of new technology, we're talking about tens of millions of jobs that could become obsolete or dramatically reduced in hours. Society *will* shift. We just don't know how yet.

But here's what I *do* know: The people who've taken the time to explore who they are, to build new skills, to create art, to think deeply, to connect meaningfully – those people are going to be a lot more ready for what's coming than those who just kept their heads down and hoped nothing would change.

Yes, you have a job today. But that doesn't mean you'll have it tomorrow. That's not doom and gloom, it's just real. And it means you have a choice:

- You can either use the time you gain to double down on the only thing you've ever known.

  OR

- You can use it to finally explore who you really are, what you're curious about, and who you want to become.

Because in the end, that's what gives you options. That's what gives you peace. That's what makes time feel *well spent.*

Diversion or Discovery

So many people are *petrified* of having time. Not just a little uncomfortable. Not mildly anxious. Petrified. Completely out of practice with what to do when there's space – when there's silence. When you're not grinding, not rushing, not scrolling.

And it shows up in the smallest, dumbest ways. I saw this post the other day: Someone was on a plane and saw a sign that said, *"All our screens are broken. Please relax and enjoy your flight."* And they posted it with this comment: *What am I going to do for 90 minutes?*

That says it all.

What do you mean, "What are you going to do?" You could take a nap. Read a book. Meditate. Reflect. Stare out the window. Think. Just take the time and be present in the moment!

But for a lot of people, that's the real nightmare.

And why?

Because we've spent our entire lives, and generations before us, never having the opportunity of what it means to just be with yourself. To have time and not immediately fill it with noise or nonsense. We've been trained to avoid stillness at all costs.

We've built our entire culture around distractions – apps, tasks, obligations, screens, reels, posts, notifications – so when time finally shows up? We panic.

We're faced with a divergent choice.

Let's say AI wipes out your job. Not just your *job*, but your whole *industry*. It's gone. And suddenly, you've got all this time.

There are two paths in front of you:

1. **Diversion** – You go full escape mode: Call of Duty, Instagram, day drinking, YouTube rabbit holes. The distractions are endless. And honestly, they're getting better and better at keeping you in them.

2. **Discovery** – You stop. You reflect. You ask hard questions. You try to figure out what fulfillment could actually look like. You begin the slow, strange, beautiful process of rebuilding your life around something real.

The problem is that diversions *feel* like connection. They *feel* like fun. But when you zoom out, most of them are ... Empty. Shallow. Forgettable.

Do you ever get one of those weekly screen time reports and feel a little sick? Yeah, you tell yourself it was mostly podcasts or audiobooks – but you're probably skipping past the two or three hours of doom scrolling. You know the ones. Instagram reels, TikToks, endlessly flicking your thumb across a glowing screen.

Some of it's genuinely funny. Genuinely creative. I'm not immune to it. I love seeing great piano players, brilliant comedy, clever pranks. It's fun. But it's also hollow.

None of that moves your life forward. The best-case scenario is you send a clip to a couple of friends and go, "LOL, check this out." But that's where it ends. There's no deeper conversation. No shared memory. It's passive consumption masquerading as connection.

And when we do have real experiences – like a trip or something actually worth talking about – we don't even talk about it anymore. We scroll. We narrate a slideshow on our phones to other people who don't really want to see 1,037 blurry shots of a building you already forgot the name of.

It's like our social muscle has atrophied.

We've forgotten how to tell stories. How to have conversations that live in the moment, that have texture and emotion and life. Now it's just data. Visual proof that something happened, as if that's more meaningful than simply sharing it with someone in real time.

But here's the thing: No photo ever replaces being there. No scroll ever replaces presence. No meme ever fills the void of a quiet evening spent alone with your thoughts, figuring out who the hell you are.

All of this – the distractions, the diversions, the endless feeding of content into our overstimulated brains – it's a facsimile of life. A glossy veneer. It feels like life. But it isn't life.

Life is time.

Time spent reflecting. Creating. Connecting. Learning. Experiencing. Feeling.

And if we keep handing all our time to diversions because we're scared of what we'll find in the quiet, then we'll never find anything at all.

So the next time you get 90 minutes to yourself, don't panic.

Be still.

Start small.

Let it be uncomfortable.

Because that's how you learn to live *fully.*

Presence and Meaning

"When you're at work, work.

When you're at the beach,

be at the beach."

– Jim Rohn

There's a meditation I love – a practice that has stuck with me, although I'll admit it's a bit morbid. It's simple: Imagine that everything you do, you will do for the last time. You'll never know when that moment will really come, but if you live every moment like your last, then you'll always be living for today – not tomorrow.

Try it.

Imagine you're sitting down for a meal, but what if this is the last time you'll ever sit down to this specific meal, in this way, with this company? Or you're spending time with your spouse, what if this is the last time you'll get to share this moment with them, in this way? The last time you wake up next to them, or the last time you kiss them goodnight?

I know it sounds a little heavy, but it's a reminder to *be present.* This awareness, this idea of the "last time," helps me cherish moments that I would normally rush through.

I think about my son, for example. He's growing out of his bike – the one he's had since he was four. He's ten now, and soon enough, he'll be riding a regular-sized bike. Maybe one day, he'll even be driving a car. There will be a last time he jumps on that small bike, just like there will be a last time he runs to greet me when I pull into the driveway. Right now, he bursts out of the back door as soon as he hears my car, running up to open my door, jumping in to give me a hug. It's the highlight of my day. But how long is that going to last? Certainly not when he's 15. Probably not even when he's 13.

These moments are fleeting. And that's what this meditation brings into sharp focus: the beauty of *right now,* and the awareness that nothing is permanent.

It's easy to get caught up in the hustle of life. Maybe you're juggling groceries or a meeting that's starting in five minutes. You pull into the driveway, and there's your kid, bursting out the door, running toward you with open arms. And in that moment, there's a voice in your head that says, *You've got things to do. You're late. You can't waste time on this right now.*

But if you take a breath, slow down, and remind yourself: *This moment will never come again.* If you're two minutes late to the meeting, it's okay. The meeting will still happen, and it's likely no one will even notice. But your kid? They'll always remember that hug, that moment you slowed down to show them that they matter.

This practice helps us to step back and really ask ourselves: "Is what I'm doing right now reinforcing who I want to be? Or is it taking me further away from that person?"

It's so easy to get distracted. The scrolling. The endless news feed. The videos that promise to entertain, but ultimately leave us feeling emptier than before. I'll admit, I enjoy it sometimes. But more and more, I find myself thinking, *Is this really helping me? Is this moving my life forward?*

We all need breaks. It's okay to indulge in the distractions. Life is meant to be enjoyed, and sometimes, that means eating the candy. But if you find yourself eating candy all day, every day, it's time for a change. You need to recognize when the diversions are taking over, and it's important to set boundaries – whether that's a timer on your phone or setting intentional breaks to do something different.

Find the balance. Enjoy the candy, but don't let it be your only diet. Create space for something more, something fulfilling.

The Art of Asking Questions

You deserve to know yourself. You deserve to feel at home in your own head. But you don't get there by accident. You get there by choosing to sit in the discomfort of silence long enough for it to transform into presence.

So, sit there in silence and reflect on these questions:

1. **The last time you had a quiet moment to yourself, what did you do with that time?**
   Did you do something creative, did you reflect, did you watch the world go by? How did it make you feel when you did that?

2. **Are there questions in your life that you've been avoiding simply because you haven't made space to hear them?**
   What kind of things could you open yourself up to if you made that space?

3. **What does "presence" mean to you – and what's getting in the way of you experiencing more of it?**
   Think beyond just work.

4. **Can you identify one area of your life where you're choosing busyness over introspection? Why might that be?**
   Really think about your answer to this one, we've talked about a lot of the possible answers already – is it one of those, or something else?

5. **If the idea of "having time" no longer scared you, what might change in your life?**
   What would you be able to face or create if you used your time more meaningfully?

This is your invitation to reclaim your time, your mind, and your peace. It's not about quitting your job or moving to a cabin in the woods; it's about creating space in your life right now to ask yourself the real questions and discover how you can live more fully.

Conclusion
Are You Ready to Start Living?

"Everyone dies but not

everyone truly lives."

– Chris Guillebeau

So if you're wondering how to begin *truly* living, start by asking yourself better questions. Not, "What should I do this weekend?" but "What have I been avoiding?" What question haven't I asked myself lately? What belief have I been holding onto without ever challenging it? What could I see differently if I were brave enough to take the opposite point of view? What kind of love or gratitude could I show someone close to me – without spending a dime?

You don't need to wait for a near-death experience to realize how precious your time is. You just need to look around.

The truth is the real fear isn't death. The real fear is that you'll never actually live. That you'll spend your time waiting – telling yourself that one day you'll get around to the things you say matter – but that day never comes. It gets buried under errands, meetings, and half-hearted weekends. You don't realize it's slipping away until it's gone.

I once heard this concept that you have your "go-go" years, your "slow-go" years, and your "no-go" years. What shocked me is how fast we move from one to the next.

A guy I know once told me a story about his parents. His mom had always wanted to travel – it was her dream. She waited for her husband to retire so they could finally go. He didn't love traveling, but he agreed to do it for her. Two weeks into retirement, he was diagnosed with stage 4 cancer. He skipped his slow-go years entirely and went straight to the no-go years. His window just closed. No warning, no decision, just gone.

My dad had a similar story. He worked for decades driving trucks, always with this one clear dream: retire, get a motorcycle, and ride across the U.S. Just him, his thoughts, the open road. Total freedom. Finally, after twenty-something years, he retired. My brother, who was stationed on an army base out West, invited him to come visit. Told him to rent a motorcycle, said he'd take him out to some beautiful camping spots.

They tried. But during just a five-day trip, my dad dropped the bike three times. Not because of a crash, just because he wasn't physically capable anymore. The strength was gone. The coordination was gone. The dream was gone, and he hadn't even realized it until it was too late. He had spent decades thinking, "I'll do that someday," only to realize that someday had quietly slipped past him without asking permission.

And that's the thing. You don't get a warning. You don't get a heads-up. You just go from thinking you'll always have time … to not having time at all.

That's why when someone calls me and says, "Can you come?" I just go. Because I know tomorrow's not promised. I know the dream deferred becomes the dream lost.

I've heard so many people, again and again, say, "I've been meaning to … I've been thinking about it for X years." And then, they say, "I'm not ready yet. I haven't figured it all out. Once I understand it better, then I'll get around to doing it." But they never do. And it breaks my heart.

Because the truth is, you *don't* have to have it all figured out. You just have to *do* it. But people get stuck in this illusion of control, thinking they can wait until the timing is perfect. They forget: The timing is never perfect. The control is never real.

So, if you're looking to truly live, stop waiting. Stop assuming there'll be more time. Show up now. Ask the hard questions now. Love harder now. Say what you need to say. Do what matters and do it *now.*

Don't wait for someday. Someday isn't guaranteed. And the cost of waiting might be everything.

Next Steps

If you're wondering what comes next, then I would encourage you, dear reader, to further explore my personal website, shanemahoney360.com. There, you may schedule time on my calendar, call me, explore my videos, connect with me on my personal and business social media accounts, read our blog, and more.

If you're inspired to begin traveling and wish to transform your travel dreams into memories, you may go to lugostravel.com and pick from any of over 75 tours in 20 countries. Look for the yellow box in each tour page and click **Get Your Itinerary** for full details in minutes.

If you're just not sure what to do next, then my advice is to go out and be okay with making mistakes … and to prove it to yourself, do something out of character and live in the moment. Embody this different you and then, later, take a step back and see how you feel.

Not every move will be the right one, but if you follow your gut, and try new things, you'll find new ways to surprise yourself and perhaps, start living a new path destined for greatness.

Testimonials

"Lugos Travel shattered my perception of what a travel company could offer. I never felt like a 'tourist' peering in from the outside; instead, I felt integrated, engaged, and inspired at every turn. For those who cherish authenticity but also appreciate the support of a professional team, Lugos Travel delivers an experience like no other.

If, like me, you thought guided tours were only for the 'other kind of traveler,' I encourage you to give Lugos Travel a chance. You might find, as I did, that they've redefined what travel can be."

– Glenn G.

"Exquisitely thoughtful, sublimely attentive, unexpectedly creative. Lugos makes you feel like you're their favorite client and like your trip is the coolest one they've ever imagined. Highly recommended."

– Dave S.

"It has been a lifelong dream to take a trip to Italy with the people I love the most. Italy is where my dad's family was from and the culture that I knew as a child. I had a budget and a vision and Shane and his team at Lugos Travel brought it to life.

I didn't know what would make an amazing experience once there, but Shane knew. And he orchestrated it perfectly! We had an ideal balance between planned activities and time to ourselves to explore. Our private tour guides made the trip! Our drivers were always on time and took great care of us.

Shane and his team took care of every detail. We are already thinking about where to go next and will certainly look to Shane and Lugos to help us create it!"

– Debbie D.

"Details, Details, Details ... make all the difference. That is why Lugos Travel and SHANE MAHONEY are the best! We had such an awesome two week vacation in Europe. Trains, planes, tickets, hotels, guides were all handled for us. Thank you Shane for a wonderful vacation!"

– Michelle G.

About the Author

Shane Mahoney is the founder and CEO of Lugos Travel, a premier luxury travel company specializing in bespoke, culturally immersive experiences. Drawing from more than a decade in the travel industry – and over 12 years in sales and finance across real estate and automotive sectors – Shane brings a rare blend of business acumen and global perspective to curating unforgettable journeys for discerning travelers.

A lifelong explorer, Shane's passion for travel began in childhood, having lived in diverse locales such as Borneo, Australia, and Spain. These formative experiences inspired his gift for uncovering the soul of each destination – something he now weaves into every tailor-made itinerary. Under his visionary leadership, Lugos Travel is known for its seamless planning, personalized service, and exclusive access to both iconic landmarks and hidden gems.

Shane is deeply driven, in all ways, to help people live their lives to the fullest, never waiting for tomorrow to pursue what matters most. Renowned as a thought leader in luxury travel, he regularly shares his insights on intentional, ethical travel and inspires others to live boldly, travel deeply, and never postpone joy.

Did You Love This Book?

* * * * *

I'd be honored if you'd share your thoughts
by leaving an honest review on Amazon!